Legendary
Guitarists
& their guitars

Acknowledgements

Dom Kiris would like to thank Paul Personne, Louis Bertignac, Stéphane Chéron, Eric Perringaux, Yazid Manou and Simone.

Gilles Verlant would like to thank Victor (guitar), Oscar (bass) and Annie (celestial vocals).

First published in the UK in 2010 by
Apple Press, 7 Greenland Street, London NW1 0ND
www.apple-press.com

ISBN 978 1 84543 385 7

© Éditions Fetjaine, 2008
An imprint of La Martinière Groupe

Title of the original edition:
Guitares et Guitaristes de Légende
Published by Éditions Fetjaine, Paris, France

Editor: Gilles Verlant

Legendary Guitarists

& their guitars

Dom Kiris

APPLE

Contents

Introduction

Whatever kind of music you listen to, from rock to pop, from folk to reggae, they all have one thing in common: the guitar. Whether it's electric or acoustic, there's no other instrument that can boast that it's been the catalyst for so many new ideas, and that it's been at the heart of so many revolutions not only in music, but also in culture and society. With blues music, the guitar was the mouthpiece for suffering minorities, then when it became electric, it became the emblem of teenage revolt. And maybe it's no coincidence that it became more powerful, in all senses of the word, at the same rate as the volume of protest went up.

This book is much more than a catalogue of beautiful guitars: its mission is to describe the links that each instrument had with the artists who made them cult objects.

So BB King's Lucille, a Gibson ES-335 whose feminine nickname sums up the king of the blues' affection for this guitar, for which he risked his life to save from a fire in a club. There's so much to say about Jimi Hendrix's Electric Lady, a Stratocaster caressed into ecstasy in the depths of the most savage brutality. Rory Gallagher sweated blood and tears on his, so much so that it became unplayable. Keith Richards and his five-string Telecaster became as one and turned into the "Human riff". Jimmy Page made the flame-top Les Paul Standard the Holy Grail of electric guitars. And let's not even start on The Beatles – whenever any one of them adopted a new instrument, it would fly off the shelf instantly, to the point where the famous Rickenbackers that they picked up during the *Help!* period quickly became known as Rickenbeatles. And then there are the musicians who create their very own instruments. Throughout his career with Queen, Brian May played his unique Red Special, which he produced himself. Eric Clapton took apart the best bits of three different Stratocasters to produce his Blackie.

When you choose your guitar, you choose your side; your distinguishing feature. Mark Knopfler yearned for the same Strato Red Fiesta as the one Hank Marvin used playing with The Shadows. Noel Gallagher adorns his semi-hollow signature model with the Union Jack as a nod to the pop culture of 1960s England.

But you don't have to be a rock star, or even a wealthy collector to treat yourself to a little piece of rock history. These days you can easily afford a scuffed replica of the Telecaster strummed by Joe Strummer, and with a bit of luck, you might even be able to get your hands on the Jag-Stang designed by Kurt Cobain.

All of the legendary guitars in this book have had such an impact on the pop culture of the last forty or fifty years that however much they want to change the world, younger generations have no desire to change guitars. In an era where the Guitar Hero avatars are taking the video game world by storm and models see them as little more than the latest fashion accessory, it's vital that we put the guitar back in its rightful place: in the hands of the guitar players. Because that's how legends are born. Play it loud!

Brian Setzer, San Francisco, 1998.

Gretsch

**Gretsch White Falcon G6136
(with Cadillac tailpiece).**

The company was founded by Friedrich Gretsch, a young 27-year-old German immigrant who opened his musical instrument shop in Brooklyn in 1883 where he sold tambourines, banjos and drum kits.

The business boomed, but Gretsch died just 12 years later, leaving the shop to be run by his young son Fred, who was still a teenager. In the young man's hands, the company grew and started to meet growing demand from its customers. The banjo era was nearing an end: the time of the guitar had arrived. The company immediately started offering good-quality guitars, and quickly made its mark in the field. In the 1940s, Gretsch was inspired by the Gibson L-5, and so the Synchromatic was born. An elegant archtop in a pre-war art-deco style, which could easily rival creations from the best guitar designers in New York including John D'Angelico and Elmer Stromberg. Gretsch's secret weapon was to ask high-profile guitarists like George Van Eps and Django Reinhardt to play on the guitars with the famous slogan: *"Great Gretsch Sound"*. But it was the advent of rock 'n' roll that would cement the brand's success in the early 1950s with the unique sound and unmistakable look.

Gretsch experienced a slight lull between 1967 and 1985 when the business was bought by British company Baldwin Manufacturing who thought they'd got a great deal when they picked it up for just $6 million. Unfortunately, the takeover coincided with the arrival of new musical trends like psychedelia, pop and hard rock, with the likes of Jimi Hendrix, Jeff Beck and Eric Clapton, which proved to be the fatal blow. It was the end of the clean, aesthetic, slightly kitsch sounds of the 1950s… The business moved to Arkansas and suffered two fires in close succession; in the 1970s, sales plummeted, until production was stopped at the beginning of the following decade.

In 1986, helped by the momentous return of rockabilly and a certain Brian Setzer (Stray Cats), who carried his Nashville Chet Atkins with him like a standard, the company returned to the family fold. At this point, Fred Gretsch III restarted production by reissuing the collections from the 1950s and 1960s as well as coming up with new models that followed in the family tradition.

Gretsch White Falcon

"The most beautiful guitar in the world!" So the White Falcon was introduced at the NAMM show in California in 1954 by its creator, Jimmie Webster. The instrument was indeed beautiful, and the most luxurious and most expensive in Gretsch's catalogue. During the 1950s, when modernity and innovation were gaining popularity, Gretsch was one of the first to offer coloured finishes: orange, green, or simple white, with the White Falcon a favourite among fans of guitar craftsmanship.

TRADE SECRETS

Jimmie Webster, whose work included demonstrating guitars for Gretsch, created the White Falcon as a prototype of the guitar of the future. It was an immaculate, dream instrument, with gold-plated mechanisms and ostentatious gold plastic. In 1955, the elegant hollow body Gretsch, available for $600, made quite a splash when it came into direct competition with the Gibson Super 400 CES. The eye can't help but be drawn to the tailpiece without a tremolo arm, nicknamed the Cadillac because of its chrome V.

With this guitar, Jimmie Webster had developed the first ever tapping technique to demonstrate the quality of DeArmond pickups. They were eventually replaced in 1958 with Filter'Tron dual coils with a richer sound.

To get the most out of his famous technique, Webster created an ingenious stereo version of the Falcon, which separated the sound of the three bass strings on one side, and the treble strings on the other, on two different amplifiers — one on the right, the other on the left!

Neil Young has a similar model, although he doesn't go for the two-hand tapping favoured by Eddie Van Halen.

Gretsch White Falcon I.

DEFINITIVE TRACKS

Mist	Jimmie Webster
Help!	George Harrison
Not Alone Any More	The Traveling Wilburys
Ohio	Crosby, Stills, Nash & Young

You would be forgiven for thinking that the glittering golden flamboyance of the White Falcon might have put off **Crosby, Stills, Nash & Young**, the four musketeers of folk. But that would be to underestimate these true lovers of beautiful rock 'n' roll guitars. Neil Young and Stephen Stills were already using vintage models when they were in Buffalo Springfield in the mid-1960s. At the beginning of the following decade, when they were touring with David Crosby and Graham Nash, you would see as many as three White Falcons on stage at any one time. Neil Young still uses his white guitar for his solo albums and tours. Since 2000, Stephen Stills has had his signature White Falcon, which is an exact replica of the 1958 model that he's had for many years.

GEORGE'S GRETSCHES

In 1960s Europe, it wasn't easy to get hold of these beautiful American guitars. **George Harrison** bought his first for $75 after answering an advertisement from a sailor who was bringing a Gretsch Duo Jet back from the States. It went everywhere with him, from the Cavern in Liverpool to the nightclubs in Hamburg, not to mention tours around Europe and America, and album recordings with The Beatles. Thanks to the exposure Harrison gave to the different models he played, on stage and on TV when he appeared with the Fab Four, Gretsch sales rocketed. George had several himself, from the Chet Atkins Country Gentleman to the Tennessean – the ultimate rockstar's guitar which he played in *Help!* But his favourite guitar was always the Duo Jet which he proudly posed with on the cover of his solo album, "Cloud Nine", which came out in the mid 1980s.

As a tribute to his Gretsch years, in 1980, George Harrison formed the supergroup, The Traveling Wilburys, alongside Jeff Lynne, Tom Petty, Roy Orbison and Bob Dylan, all of whom played with vintage models. Quite a coup for the Gretsch family's return to business in 1989. The first guitar that was produced when the company reopened was a limited edition three-quarter size model with a copy of the stars' signatures on the back, and a unique design for every instrument.

Gretsch 6120

The 1950s was a golden age for the company thanks in no small part to the advent of the rock 'n' roll era, during which the hearts of American youngsters began to beat a little faster. Gretsch rode the wave of the rise of the electric guitar by offering the perfect model to bridge the gap between country, jazz and rock 'n' roll: the supreme 6120, with its striking orange finish and hollow body, designed by Chet Atkins himself. Available in two models – Nashville or Tennessean – it epitomises the ultimate rockabilly guitar.

Gretsch 6120
Chet Atkins
(1955).

© Pictorial/DALLE

TRADE SECRETS

The 6120 model, which came out in 1954 costing $385, branded with the letter G, reminiscent of cattle branding in the dusty Far West plains — clearly this was an instrument that was unashamedly aimed at the country market! The neck is adorned with cacti, longhorns and mother-of-pearl horseshoes on some models. The look is always crucial for Gretsch, and the finishes are painstakingly designed. The laminated maple body, sides and tailored soundboard are brought out by a thick layer of translucent varnish that gives it its characteristic orange colour. As is typical of hollow bodies, the f-holes are particularly wide which really let the sound breathe. The DeArmond pickups fitted on the first models were replaced by Filter-Trons in 1957, inspired by the humbuckers made by Gibson. The sound is so mellow and round that you can just picture Gene Vincent's quiff as he gets stuck into a rockabilly riff. The great style icons of rock 'n' roll are huge fans of the 6120, with its narrow and incredibly comfortable neck. The tremolo arm is a genuine bigsby. Paul Bigsby was a handyman who was mad about motors and music, and in 1948 he created a tremolo effect for Merle Travis with a special tailpiece that could vary the tension in the strings thanks to a cylindrical bar and a spring. After they are pulled taught, they return to their original position without going out of tune (well, most of the time...). Most Gretsch guitars were fitted with one from the 1950s onwards.

NEW

NOW INCLUDES THIS FANTASTIC **LEGO** CREMATORIUM!

LEGO

Options · Share · Like

Christopher Hurton

Andrew Letby shared Andy Wright's photo.
30 November at 17:54 via Mobile ·

LEGO
Funeral Directors
Play set
part of the [FUN WITH MORTALITY] range
ages 4-10
www.lego.co.uk
NEW
NOW INCLUDES THIS FANTASTIC LEGO CREMATORIUM!

LEGO
Funeral Directors
Play Set
part of the [FUN WITH MORTALITY] range
ages
4-10
TWO NEW FIGURES!

Like · 893 people like this.

Bit When You're Born

My world this
Like · Share
46 people
331 share

Mark Hockn 28 Nov

Ed Ho 28 Nov

An Sut

Guitar Heroes

In the mid-1950s, **Chet Atkins**, nicknamed Mister Guitar, was already at the top of his game in the musical world, in Nashville and further afield. He started out in the 1940s with the Carter Family, then became a radio star with his famous picking style, inspired by Merle Travis. After he was signed up by RCA, in 1956 he produced recording sessions with Elvis Presley for *Heartbreak Hotel* before he took over the prestigious label himself. Like Les Paul, whom he greatly admired and with whom his brother Jim had played as part of a trio, Chet Atkins made his dream guitar with the generously proportioned 6120.

Eddie Cochran is a rock 'n' roll legend, immortalised in the film *The Girl Can't Help It* in 1956 in which he was seen singing with his 6120. The scene resulted in him being signed up by the Liberty label and he went on to record hits including *Summertime Blues* and *C'mon Everybody* – timeless classics loved by generations of music lovers.
Recordings by this brilliant guitarist, composer and arranger still sound incredibly fresh and modern half a century later. He was one of the pioneers of the rockabilly style with his 1955 Gretsch and gold bigsby tremolo arm and the addition of a Gibson P-90 pickup next to the neck.
His career bloomed with toe-tapping songs that sent girls wild and inspired young men. He could have overshadowed Elvis, but it was not to be as he died in a car accident on 17th April 1960 during a hugely successful tour of England with Gene Vincent. He was just 21 years old. His spirit lived in on in other fans of the Gretsch 6120 including a certain Brian Setzer.

It was as a nod to Cochran, his absolute idol, that **Brian Setzer** bought his first 6120 at the end of the 1970s for $100 in a store in Long Island, New York, where he was born in 1959. This Gretsch, which dated back to the year of his birth, was introduced on the first mind-blowing album by the Stray Cats, which made rockabilly fashionable again in the 1980s. Adorned with stickers of pin-ups and a scruffy black cat (which had given the band its name), this western guitar had pretty much gone into retirement before it was given a new lease of life in the hands of this genius. Setzer had certainly earned his unmistakable signature guitar with its volume and tone knobs in the shape of dice. He also breathed new life into the sound with TV Jones or Hot Rod Filter'Tron pickups.

Duane Eddy was one of the original rock 'n' roll *guitar heroes*: he has sold more than 100 million instrumental records showcasing the characteristic twang of his guitar. This distinctive sound was discovered when Duane was with his producer Lee Hazlewood and had the idea of running his amplifier from the 6120 through an old tank that had been rescued from a rubbish dump. By focusing on the low notes, he managed to produce a sound full of echoes and tremolo to create a striking effect that would launch the surf guitar trend and inspire many a guitar hero including Link Wray and Hank Marvin from The Shadows.
"My '57 red Gretsch has been part of the Duane Eddy sound since the day I got it, he admitted when he was inducted into the Rock 'n' Roll Hall of Fame in 1994.

Gretsch G6120
Brian Setzer.

Definitive Tracks

Tennessee Stud	Chet Atkins
Twenty Flight Rock	Eddie Cochran
Rock This Town	The Stray Cats
Peter Gunn	Duane Eddy

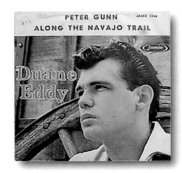

Gretsch Bo Diddley

Bo Diddley didn't just create a rock 'n' roll style that drew on his African roots – he also invented his very own instruments in all sorts of weird and wonderful shapes.
To celebrate the tireless Road Runner's 70th birthday, Gretsch reissued the first blazing red rectangular guitar, which was originally made in 1958. It was part of the Electromatic Signature collection, model name G5810.
Diddley was never happy to buy an instrument from a shop. All of his guitars were homemade even back when he was a kid on the streets, whiling away time playing on a piece of wire string stretched over a wooden board with a bottleneck: the Diddley Bow, which presumably gave rise to his nickname. Unless it came from his days in the ring as a boxer!

Gretsch Bo Diddley.

Gretsch 6120 Chet Atkins (1955)

DEFINITIVE TRACKS

Who Do You Love	Bo Diddley
I'm a Man	Bo Diddley
Road Runner	Bo Diddley

Guitar Heroes

Elias McDaniel, was born in 1928 in McComb, Mississippi and died in 2008. He was more than just a musician: he was a groundbreaking pioneer.

"Elvis is King, but **Bo Diddley** is Daddy", said Tom Petty during the celebrations for the legend's 50th anniversary in the business in 2005. His first hit, *I am a Man*, along with the autobiographical A-side *Bo Diddley* was released by Chess Records and made quite a splash. The jungle sound was born: one chord repeated over and over, in a hypnotic rhythm. Maracas, tambourines and tribal drums accompany a demonic guitar riff combined with tremolo and fuzz effects.

"I was the very first one to start to change the sound of the electric guitar into what is now called rock 'n' roll", claimed the man who was imitated and emulated by the younger generations through the 1960s. The first in a long line, the Rolling Stones had their first real hit with *Not Fade Away*, an inspired song credited to Buddy Holly.

Bo Diddley on stage in Memphis in 2006 with his legendary Gretsch.

TRADE SECRETS

Most of these extraordinary guitars — square, rectangular or covered in fur — are assembled by famous luthier Tom Holmes who was also known for the guitars that he created for Billy Gibbons and ZZ Top. The ones he made for Bo Diddley are characterised by their authentic blues feel and the spirit of the first rudimentary instruments made from cigar boxes…

Guild

The prestigious American label, Guild, has a rich history, brimming with personalities and innovation. It is well known for the quality of its acoustic guitars, which are in the same league as the creations of Gibson and Martin.

Guild was founded in 1952 by Alfred Dronge, a Polish Jew who grew up in New York. A brilliant musician and jazz lover, he played professionally and gave guitar lessons before making his fortune by importing Italian accordions.

With this new taste for business, he created his own business with George Mann, a former executive at Epiphone. They chose the name Guild as a nod to associations of craftsmen in the Middle Ages.

Starting in a modest workshop in Manhattan, the company grew to become a major manufacturer, with luthiers recruited from Gretsch and Epiphone, producing (archtop) jazz guitars to order. The strategy soon paid off: four years later, the first factory was opened in New Jersey. Sales boomed and partnership contracts were signed with fashionable guitarists like jazzman Johnny Smith, known for his hit *Moonlight in Vermont*, for which the Artist Award was created. For the rock 'n' roll world, Guild produced the DE-400 for the king of twang, Duane Eddy. In the 1960s,

Guild pre-empted the rise in popularity of folk music. The D (for *dreadnought*) range of acoustic guitars with six or 12 strings was popular with famous musicians including Richie Havens, whose performance at Woodstock with his D-40 secured its legendary status.

In 1966, Guild was bought by electronic giants, Avnet, who moved manufacturing to Rhode Island. Al Dronge stayed on at the helm but in 1972, he died in an accident in the aeroplane that he flew to travel for his work. The company continued to prosper in spite of this loss: production expanded to include electric guitars and basses. After a difficult period in the 1980s and several changes of ownership, Guild was bought by Fender in 1995 who gave it a new image by refocusing its efforts on quality acoustic guitars.

Richie Havens' signature Guild D-40.

Guild D-40

DEFINITIVE TRACKS

Freedom	Richie Havens
Here Comes the Sun	Richie Havens
Moonlight in Vermont	Johnny Smith

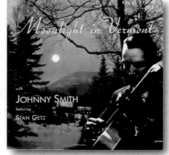

Guild has produced *dreadnought* guitars inspired by Martin's since 1963. They played an important role in the 1960s Folk revival. The D-40 is a powerful guitar that holds chords perfectly and handles any rhythm effortlessly – the perfect partner for a guitarist and his plectrum. The original models (the D-40 and D-50) were reissued at the beginning of 2000 as the Bluegrass Jubilee D-40 or the Special Jubilee D-50.

© Knight-Redferns/DALLE

Jubilee D-40.

Legendary American folk singer **Richie Havens** had his big break at Woodstock in the August of 1969. Alone on the stage with his acoustic Guild D-40, he opened the festival by playing for nearly three hours straight, finishing his set with a memorable rendition of a song that went on to become known as *Freedom*.

Born in Brooklyn, Richie Havens started out busking with doo wop and gospel songs before he started learning to play the guitar and moved to Greenwich Village. Ensconced in the 1960s folk scene, he met Bob Dylan whose songs he would go on to sing. With a deep, seasoned voice, Havens has been singing about peace and brotherly love for more than forty years (his last album, "Nobody Left to Crown", came out in 2008). Richie Havens has had his own Guild signature model since 2003. His D-40 has two plastic pickguards designed to protect it from his right hand with his open-D tuning. He bars the chords with just his thumb: "I tried learning the "straight" way, but my fingers are so large that when I put them down I hit two strings at once. And it's a great way of singing any kind of folk song."

TRADE SECRETS

The solid design of the D-40 gives it total balance. The combination of different woods — the spruce sound board, the mahogany back and sides — give it a warm, rootsy sound in the low notes and a clear, true one in the high notes. It's also perfect for a bluesy picking style thanks to its comfortable mahogany neck. The fingerboard and bridge of the D-40 are made of rosewood, and its natural finish gives it real class, with its wide tortoiseshell pickguard protecting it from over-enthusiastic plectrums. In 1968, its little sister, the D-55, was given a sunburst finish, initially for a one-off order, but it was so popular with country singers like Waylon Jennings that it's been in the catalogue ever since.

The Red Special

**The Red Special is Brian May's guitar, which he made himself. Queen's very own guitar hero honed his craft as he built his instrument, and it is almost exclusively this guitar that he has used throughout a career that has spanned more than forty years, both on stage and in the recording studio.
Hank Marvin from The Shadows, who was Brian May's idol as a teenager, with the Red Special in his hands, thought it was an enigmatic but ultimately fascinating instrument.**

TRADE SECRETS

Brian May was born in Hampton, England in 1947. At school he excelled in science and was passionate about music. In 1963 during his summer holidays, he decided to make his very own electric guitar with the help of his father who was an electronics engineer.

Most of the wood came from an 18th century oak fireplace. From this extremely hard wood, riddled with wormholes, he hand-carved the neck of the guitar.

The sound box is covered in plywood and two sheets of mahogany, making it look like a solid-body guitar while it was in fact a semi-acoustic one with a unique, open sound.

The whole thing was homemade using second-hand materials. The position inlays are mother-of-pearl buttons borrowed from Mrs May's sewing box; Brian made the tremolo system himself from an old hardened-steel knife blade and a couple of motorbike valve springs which were then mounted on a bicycle saddle bag holder and held in place with a plastic knitting needle. And it works! The pickups are Burns Tri-Sonics rewound with a switch so that the three pickups could be used at the same time, and reverse polarity offering a broader range of sounds. Hand-painted red, then covered in several layers of plastic coating to protect it, it justifiably earned the nickname the Red Special.

The guitar was eighteen long months in the making, but cost just £17.50.

Guitar Heroes

Thanks in no small part to his unique instrument, **Brian May** is one the most easily identifiable guitarists in the history of rock. He uses super-thin strings which he plays with a pre-decimal sixpence piece, so he can attack the notes, which he modulates gracefully thanks to his mastery of vibrato. He also likes to pick big fat saturated chords on his Vox amp for hits like *We Will Rock You*. "I'm just a kid with a guitar", he explains – nothing's changed in forty years! The zenith of his talent can be heard on *Bohemian Rhapsody*, a song in which his instrumental virtuosity, interwoven with the soaring vocals of Freddie Mercury, created a symphonic rock masterpiece: simply phenomenal. Another good example is *Killer Queen*, which flaunts his talents as an arranger, with classical influences and a stunning solo performed on his Red Special.

REPRODUCTIONS

After thirty years of intensive use, Brian decided to get his Red Special produced by Greg Fryer, an Australian luthier who had already built him models similar to the original one. The mythical guitar's little sisters were sold by Guild between 1983 and 1991, and then by Burns, who made them in Korea. Brian May wasn't happy with these cheap models, so he took over the process himself, producing excellent quality guitars under his own brand.

DEFINITIVE QUEEN TRACKS

"The Game"	(album)
Bohemian Rhapsody	("A Night at the Opera")
We Will Rock You	("News of the World")
Killer Queen	("Sheer Heart Attack")

John Scofield signature JSM100.

Paul Stanley
(Kiss) signature
PS10 Iceman.

Pat Metheny signature PM120.

Ibanez

Don't be misled by their name: Ibanez guitars are in fact produced by Hoshino Gakki in Nagoya, the third biggest city in Japan when it comes to business.
When it was founded in 1908, the company was a music bookstore that began sell musical instruments. It produced its first guitars in the 1930s when it bought the rights to use the name of famous Spanish luthier Salvador Ibanez (1854–1920).

Hoshino Gakki was badly affected by bombing in the Second World War, so it started to focus on importing and exporting reasonably priced electric guitars with unusual designs.
In 1965, attracted by the excellent value-for-money offered by the Ibanez brand, whose name evoked the grand tradition of Spanish guitars, the American company Elger Guitars rose to the challenge of distributing Japanese models in their own country. This partnership led to the creation of Ibanez USA and the launch of a concerted effort to produce copies of American guitars like Fender, Gibson and Rickenbacker. The market was soon flooded with guitars at a price that defied all competition. After all, didn't most of us start out with a replica? Ibanez can be credited with bringing the electric guitar to the masses, bringing it within the reach of youngsters who couldn't afford an original.
This spirit of philanthropy wasn't shared by the Norlin Corporation, Gibson's new owner, who took Ibanez to court for plagiarism. Hoshino Gakki lost the case, but made a comeback with original models which raised its profile, mainly by associations with well-known artists. And so it was that in the mid-1970s, Bob Weir, guitarist with the Grateful Dead, gave his name to a Cowboy Fancy, with its Western design and a multitude of knobs; Kiss guitarist Paul Stanley picked the black PS10 to go with the rest of his look.
The Japanese brand collaborated with musicians with a reputation for professionalism, including masters of modern jazz like George Benson, John Scofield and Pat Metheny, not to mention virtuosos like Steve Vai and Joe Satriani, to contribute to the guitar revival in the 1980s.

The DiMarzio pickup

Larry DiMarzio invented the super distortion pickup which accompanied the evolution of guitar players at the dawn of the 1980s. DiMarzio was both a guitar player and an electronics student who used to do repairs for shops on Manhattan's 48th Street to make a bit of money. He understood the problems encountered by musicians when it came to making a big noise in crowded clubs without turning the amp up too high. The idea was to prolong the sustain phase using the guitar. Theoretically, a guitar pickup is a very simple piece of kit: it's a battery wrapped in wire, which produces a magnetic field when it's hit by the vibration of the string. DiMarzio came up with the trick of using ceramic magnets used in hi-fi speakers with a really high output level as well as a very fine wire so that the coil can be very tightly wound. These high saturation pickups were an immediate hit with musicians.
DiMarzio was the only person to come up with different formats of pickup which could be adapted to different models of guitar. The likes of Yngwie Malmsteen, Steve Morse and most memorably Steve Vai and Joe Satriani all used them to give their Ibanez guitars a boost.

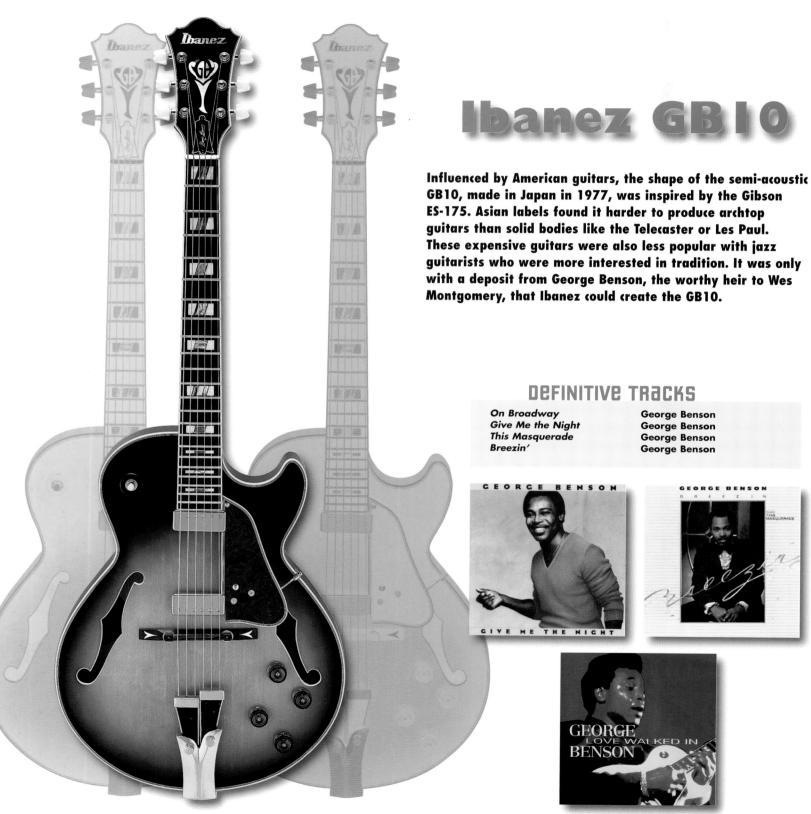

Ibanez GB10

Influenced by American guitars, the shape of the semi-acoustic GB10, made in Japan in 1977, was inspired by the Gibson ES-175. Asian labels found it harder to produce archtop guitars than solid bodies like the Telecaster or Les Paul. These expensive guitars were also less popular with jazz guitarists who were more interested in tradition. It was only with a deposit from George Benson, the worthy heir to Wes Montgomery, that Ibanez could create the GB10.

DEFINITIVE TRACKS

On Broadway	George Benson
Give Me the Night	George Benson
This Masquerade	George Benson
Breezin'	George Benson

George Benson's reputation as a brilliant guitarist is well-deserved. He has been playing with great musicians since he was a teenager, from organist Jack McDuff, who launched his career, to Miles Davies who asked him to play on his album "Miles in the Sky".

With his funky rhythms and jazz solos, he earned jazz music's first ever platinum record with "Breezin'" in 1976. He was also a gifted singer, demonstrated by his scat-accompanied improvised instrumentals.

The GB10 was first produced in 1977 – a flexible guitar that was perfect for Benson's jazz-funk playing. Capable of rounded warmth as well as sharper sounds, it was an undeniable success for the massive hit, *Give Me the Night*, produced by Quincy Jones in 1980, which made the whole world get up and dance.

George Benson, 1988.

TRADE SECRETS

The GB10 was the first instrument produced by Ibanez to carry an artist's signature. George Benson chose an electric acoustic archtop model with a thick spruce sound board and a maple back and sides. The semi-hollow body is slightly smaller and narrower than traditional jazz guitars and defines the notes perfectly, avoiding too much resonance, which can cause feedback. The two floating GB Special humbucker pickups, designed in collaboration with Benson, produce a warm, rounded sound.

The neck is fitted with an ebony fingerboard and goes down very well with fans of sliding. The height-adjustable bridge is also made of ebony. The real innovation is in the two-part tailpiece so the three low strings can be adjusted separately from the three high ones.

There is also the GB15 with a single pickup, and the GB200 with a larger standard sound box.

George Benson's name is engraved on the neck on the 21st fret, corroborating the authenticity of this ultimate groove machine!

Ibanez JS

Joe Satriani's passion for jazz began when he was a young boy, and his first forays into guitar playing involved taking Jimi Hendrix to pieces. He worked tirelessly on speed-related techniques which helped him become a teacher at Berkeley College in California. The talented instructor of greats, including Steve Vai and Kirk Hammett (Metallica), naturally needed his own guitar. And so it was that in 1990, the JS was born: a stunning, curvaceous model with the fastest neck west of the Pecos...

TRADE SECRETS

Satriani didn't have any fixed ideas apart from the configuration of the pickups and the shape of the neck, which needed to be as comfortable as possible. He couldn't have hoped for anything better: a lethal weapon for tapping, legato or the latest tricks developed by Professor Satchafunkilus.

The light, streamlined basswood body make it an incredibly supple instrument to play. The fingerboard and frets are polished to within an inch of their life because precision is key for this six-string maestro who reinvented the rock guitar genre with his instrumental albums including "Surfing with the Alien" in 1987.

No need for useless gimmicks: just a pair of DiMarzio pickups controlled by three potentiometers which give it its heavily saturated sound, plus the Edge Pro tremolo arm, patented by Ibanez. The rest was down to Satriani's five fingers, giving him an unfair advantage over us mere humans!

The only luxury that the maestro afforded himself was a silvery JS10th, affectionately nicknamed Chrome Boy, which dazzled audiences with its shimmering reflections whenever it appeared on stage.

Guitar Heroes

In the 1980s, the term *shredding* was created to describe incredibly fast and particularly dexterous playing. **Joe Satriani**, aka The Satch, epitomised the technique.

But Satriani can do anything. Who else could have been picked to replace Jeff Beck at the drop of a hat for Mick Jagger's solo tour in 1989, or Ritchie Blackmore with Deep Purple in Japan in 1994… ?

As the last millennium came to a close, Saint Joe, who must have been starting to get a bit bored, gathered together his best disciples for G3: Steve Vai, Eric Johnson, Yngwie Malmsteen, John Petrucci and Patrick Rondat are just some of the names that have appeared in the line-up. If you're going to go *head-to-head* with his JS, only a truly legendary guitar is going to come out of it alive!

DEFINITIVE TRACKS

Cool #9	Joe Satriani
Summer Song	Joe Satriani
Surfing with the Alien	Joe Satriani
Big Bad Moon	Joe Satriani

Ibanez JEM

The JEM was created by Steve Vai, one of the guitar virtuosos of the 1980s. Was it because of some kind of modesty – not really his style – that he didn't want his name to appear on it? He preferred the JEM Guitar named after the company owned by his friend the designer Joe Despagni, with whom he had been coming up with prototypes for crazy guitars ever since his first solo album "Flex-Able" in 1984.

JEM7 – JEM77 – JEM777

Vai obviously has a thing about the number 7. Take "The 7th Song – Enchanting Guitar Melodies" – an unusual greatest hits, which includes the seventh track of all of his albums (generally ballads). Then of course there's the seven-string guitar, the Ibanez Universe, which was specially designed for his standout album, "Passion and Warfare". The seventh string was a bass one that really added to the texture of the low notes. The seven-string guitar went on to be adopted by hardcore death metal fans.

DEFINITIVE TRACKS

The Audience Is Listening	Steve Vai
For the Love of God	Steve Vai
Little Green Man	Steve Vai
The Attitude Song	Steve Vai

Guitar Heroes

Born in Long Island in 1960, **Steve Vai** spent his youth studying music with a teacher who was hardly any older than he was: Joe Satriani. He went on to hone his craft with Frank Zappa who nicknamed him the "Stunt Guitarist" when he was just 19 years old. But Steve Vai made a name for himself before a wider audience when he stood up to hard-rock guitar heroes, accompanying the likes of David Lee Roth post-Van Halen and Whitesnake with David Coverdale, formerly of Deep Purple fame.

© Alary/DALLE

TRADE SECRETS

When he was coming up with the design of the JEM, Steve Vai brought together everything he liked about other guitars. When Ibanez's designer Rich Lasner presented him with the first finished model, Vai didn't play it immediately. He began by taking it apart and examining every single part. A genuine connoisseur! The body is made of American alder, which is light but dense, helping to sustain the sound. The three pickups are DiMarzio Evolutions, which are specially produced to get the distinctive super distorted sound. Then there's the double-locking tremolo arm, based on a design patented by Floyd Rose, making dexterous acrobatics possible and thus earning it its reputation. He was inspired by his old Stratocasters to come up with a thrusting design with two long pointed horns stretching far down the neck to get to the high notes. He added the famous Monkey Grip — nobody really knows what it's for but it gives the JEM its unmistakable look. The whole thing can be decorated in bright colours or a striking floral design, whichever you prefer.

Martin

Although Martin didn't exactly invent the good old acoustic guitar, he did pretty much write the rulebook. The shape, size, wood, X-bracing and the length of the neck were basically standardised by Martin guitars.

An anomaly in these times of globalisation, Martin has been a family company since its origins, run by six generations of Martins over more than 175 years.

Founder, Christian Frederick Martin (1796-1873) left his family in Germany when he was 15 years old to go and learn his trade with renowned Austrian luthier Johann Stauffer. With nothing more than his skill, he emigrated to New York in 1833 and opened his very own guitar workshop. Six years later, he opened a branch in Nazareth, Pennsylvania, where Martin's head office and factory have remained to this day.

The first models were heavily influenced by his European teacher. He made small guitars with curved lines and tuning mechanisms on one side. The idea was taken up by Leo Fender when he designed the Telecaster in 1949. His grandson, Frank Henry Martin, took over the business in 1888. At the age of 22, he embarked on Martin's first commercial venture, targeting retailers directly. From then on, it was all about money, and all the Martin heirs would go to university to learn how to run a business, right through to C. F. Martin IV, who has been at the helm since 1986.

The 000-15 and the 00-15.

Martin 000

Martin guitars are available in different models, which are named according to their size: the first 0 (zero) was created in 1850, the 00 (double zero) from 1870 onwards. It wasn't until 1902 that a 000 (triple zero) appeared. Feeling that the quadruple zero would lack elegance, the name *Dreadnought*, for D models, was inspired by the Royal Navy's battleship for the largest guitar in the catalogue. The second part of the name indicates the kind of wood used and the level of decoration: 000-15 for models made entirely of mahogany and without any ornaments, 000-45 for the deluxe model.

Guitar Heroes

Jimmie Rodgers, widely regarded as the pioneer of country music, had his very own 000-45 model in 1928: the Blue Yodel, named after one of his hit songs.

Working as a labourer for a rail company, Rodgers gave up everything to pursue his passion for music when he was diagnosed with tuberculosis. His first album, "Blue Yodel", recorded for RCA Victor in 1927, was very well received. Rodgers had an emotional style, Delta blues punctuated with a yodel at the end of each couplet. He had learnt the art of yodelling as a young boy from a Tyrolean family living in the Appalachian Mountains.

The reissued 000-45 Jimmie Rodgers, in keeping with the original, is made of Brazilian rosewood (the king of wood) for the back and the sides, with sound board

made of Adirondack spruce, considered to be the Holy Grail of sound boards.

The western style suits it well, with his name on the neck, the name, *Blue Yodel*, on the headstock and a great big *Thanks* on the back. Very hard to find, even if you can afford to pay around $25,000!

Convinced that his musical career was all planned out, the young Robert Zimmerman left his family home and made his way to Minneapolis in 1959. There he changed his name to **Bob Dylan**. "The first thing I did was swap my electric guitar for a Martin 00", he explains in his *Chronicles*. In coffee houses filled with students, Dylan discovered the world of folk, and in no time at all, he'd picked up some two hundred songs by the great Woody Guthrie. When he heard that his idol was seriously ill, he hitchhiked to New York and headed straight to Guthrie's bedside, guitar in hand. Deeply moved by the meeting, he wrote *Song to Woody* as a tribute to the old master, one of the first songs he'd ever written. His first Martin is now on show at the Experience Music Museum in Seattle.

A brilliant composer, singer and guitarist, **Stephen Stills** is one of the forefathers of Californian pop, as a member of legendary groups including Buffalo Springfield and Crosby, Stills, Nash & Young. A keen collector of vintage guitars, he's been known to take up to 17 on stage at a time. Martin seized the opportunity to pay tribute to him with his very own signature 000-45S.

It was just like the one he was playing in the snow on the sleeve of his stunning first solo album which came out in 1970, with guests including Eric Clapton and Jimi Hendrix. Stills has been playing a Martin for over forty years now, both on stage and in the studio. At his request, the company started reproducing the little acoustic 0-45 since July 2007, which he uses to compose his songs at home. Hard to refuse such a faithful client a new signature model…

Martin 000-45S signature Stephen Stills.

TRADE SECRETS

We have Martin to thank for a major innovation in flat-top acoustic guitars: in the 1840s, Christian Frederick invented the X-bracing, which involved strips of wood criss-crossing the sound board. The aim of this system is to protect the sound board from distortion and distribute the energy produced by the strings. It also corrects the tone. The more finely constructed the bracing is, the sharper the high notes are, and the deeper the low notes. The technique is still used by Martin today, as well as by most other luthiers. The invention first appeared on the 0 model in 1850. In around 1930, Martin

designed a bridge with a reinforced central piece, called the "belly bridge", either in ebony or rosewood, which would become standard on all folk guitars. At the same time, the OM (Orchestra Model) was launched with a longer neck connecting the sound box to the 14th fret. The success of this long neck, which made it easier to reach the higher notes, led the company to use it on all of its guitars. This too was copied by other manufacturers.

Martin 000-15.

Martin Dreadnought

Martin D-18.

Martin D-28.

Martin D-28.

This is without a doubt one of the most important guitars in the history of rock. Elvis Presley, The Beatles, the Rolling Stones – the list could go on for pages – have all used a Dreadnought in the recording studio, usually the D-28.

The shape of the Dreadnought, with its square shoulders, wide waist and deep body, has become the template for steel-string acoustic guitars for all manufacturers. In 1906, the Royal Navy demonstrated its might to the world with the most intimidating warship ever built: *HMS Dreadnought*. The message was clear: such a big beast wasn't afraid of anything. Martin borrowed the name for the biggest guitar in its catalogue. Its immense power, with deep bass notes and unrivalled sound projection, made it a classic acoustic guitar.

TRADE SECRETS

Strangely enough, the Dreadnought guitar didn't have the Martin name to begin with. It was first produced by the Oliver Ditson Company in Boston in 1916. The first models, the D-1 and D-2, slightly more oblong with a 12-fret neck, were produced by Martin, but as prototypes for the distributor. Once the manufacturing process had been finalised, as demand increased, Martin began distributing the Dreadnought under its own name in around 1930 with the D-28 and D-18.

When the catgut strings were replaced with steel ones, the manufacturers needed to strengthen the body to cope with the tension of the strings on the sound box. The D-18, with its solid sitka top and mahogany sides and back, is more rudimentary and lacking in ornamentation, but it is no less a classic Martin; the D-28 has a more carefully designed finish with binding that underlines the contours of the sold sitka top. The back and sides are made of Brazilian rosewood and its fingerboard and bridge are ebony. A combination of rich woods with the perfect sound for robust rhythms. The Martin Dreadnought was quickly picked up by country artists, and went on to become the perfect guitar for accompanying a wide variety of singing styles.

Guitar Heroes

Hank Williams, the greatest singer-songwriter in the history of country music, recorded most of his hits with a 1940s D-28 which was 100% handmade.

A beautiful instrument decorated in a style referred to as Old Herringbone, it had a pearly edging around the body and the sound hole. His influence was huge, and all the big names in country music, including Willy Nelson and Johnny Cash, have covered his songs. "I get more kick out of writing than I do singing", he said in 1952, just a few months before his death. "I reckon I've written a thousand songs and had over 300 published." With 12 number ones, starting with *Move it on Over* in 1947, the Hillbilly Shakespeare changed the face of traditional country songs by drawing on honky tonk (named after the bars where the style became popular) and pure country blues, without the sentimentality favoured by his contemporaries, preferring a hard-nosed realism: "I'll never get out of this world alive!" Behind the clean-cut, funfair cowboy image hid quite a party animal, hooked on booze, amphetamines and other dangerous substances. On New Year's Day 1953, Hank Williams was discovered unconscious in the back of the Cadillac in which he was being driven to his next concert. He was just 29 years old. A great admirer of the man and his guitar, Neil Young has owned one of his D-28s for more than thirty years, as he explains before singing *This Old Guitar* in Jonathan Demme's 2006 film *Heart of Gold*.

In 1998, to celebrate the 75th anniversary of Hank Williams' birth, Martin produced 150 numbered D-28HW models.

Martin D-45GA Gene Autry.

Gene Autry

The star of an unbelievable number of cowboy films produced in Hollywood in the 1930s and 1940s, Gene Autry really did start out working as a cowherd before he started his singing career, imitating Jimmie Rodgers' yodelling style.

Martin designed the D-45 especially for him in 1933 – the most deluxe guitar in its catalogue. The famous "singing cowboy" wanted the same Martin 000-45 as his idol Jimmie Rodgers, but with the new Dreadnought style. Highly sought after by collectors, only 91 copies of this model were ever produced between 1933 and 1942. Due to popular demand, the D-45 was reissued in 1968 with painstakingly produced ornamentations: it took a good 20 hours just to set the 900 pearls that adorn it!

© Gruhn Guitars

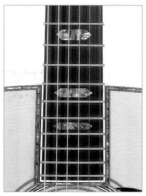

Martin D-45.

DEFINITIVE TRACKS

Back in the Saddle Again	Gene Autry
Hurt	Johnny Cash
I'm So Lonesome I Could Cry	Hank Williams
That's All Right	Elvis Presley
This Old Guitar	Neil Young

ELVIS PRESLEY

The D-18 acquired its legendary status when it first appeared with Elvis Presley in 1954–1955.

When he was recording with Sun Records in Memphis, Tennessee, Elvis bought his first Martin from O.K. Houck, a shop just down the road from the studio on Union Avenue. It was where every musician in town went, from Ike Turner to B. B. King, not to mention Johnny Cash. Specialists authenticated Presley's D-18 with the letters ELVI stuck on the spruce top: Elvis' energetic playing style allegedly caused the letter S to fall off! His guitarist Scotty Moore admitted that the young King broke a lot of strings and used to beat out the rhythm on the body. This particular Martin, tested to the max, was sold at auction by Christie's for $150,000 before it joined the Rock 'n' Roll Hall of Fame Museum in 1998 as one of the first ever instruments used for the genre.

JOHNNY CASH

To celebrate Johnny Cash's rebellious spirit, Martin finished its first guitar in polished black after favouring a natural wood colour for all its other models.

But how could they resist this non-conformist who had been faithful to his D-35 for his 20-year career? With the Black Martin, Johnny Cash recorded albums produced by Rick Rubin who introduced him to alternative rock audiences who had, until then, steered clear of country music. This was the icing on the cake of a career spanning 40 years, starting with the Sun label in 1955 alongside the likes of Elvis Presley and Jerry Lee Lewis, with 1,500 songs recorded, 48 hit singles and 11 Grammy Awards! On 12th September 2003, aged 71, Johnny Cash went from being a country icon to a legend of popular American music. Martin paid tribute to him with the D-35 Black signature model. Unluckily, the vocal cords of the Man in Black didn't come with it…

Gibson

For over a century, the Gibson name has been king in the history of the guitar, making its mark in all genres of popular music. The story began in the 19th century with Orville Gibson, and nobody has looked back since.

Orville Gibson was born in 1856, in Chateaugay (New York) to a family who had emigrated from England. Orville's twin passions were music and woodwork. He opened his workshop in Kalamazoo in Michigan in around 1880. He used to take apart old furniture made of walnut or maple, both hard, solid woods, to make mandolins. He would carve out rounded sound boards from solid pieces of wood, modelling them on European violins such as the great Stradivarius. The process lived on, becoming popular with the whole range of jazz guitars.

His patented design for the shape of his mandolins and his reputation for excellent craftsmanship caught the eye of manufacturers. The first Gibson company was formed in 1902, with Orville acting as a consultant.

Like many great creative minds, he was rather temperamental and not always well suited to business; however, his vision was crucial

to the company's success. After he died of chronic endocarditis on 19th August 1918, the company went into decline.

Everything changed with the arrival of mandolin expert Lloyd Loar. This brilliant composer, arranger and sound engineer pooled all of his talents to make sure production started again in 1919. He put the finishing touches to the carefully carved pieces of wood, borrowing the f-shaped sound holes from violins and using them on guitars and mandolins, using them for the first time on a fretted instrument with L-5 guitars and F-5 mandolins.

From this point on, the company blossomed, expanding its workshops and building a factory in Kalamazoo, Gibson's historic home. It was no coincidence that the company set up a permanent base for itself in the woody Michigan region, with its vast forests and the best carpenters around!

Thus began a magical period of innovation which would accompany the development of popular music through the 20th century, from country, jazz and blues to rock 'n' roll and pop. It's impossible to say whether the instrument or the music came first, but Gibson has always been on top of its game, honouring its slogan – "Made by musicians for musicians" – for over a century.

Orville Gibson.

The mandolin

This powerful mandolin, typical of country music, was the starting point for bluegrass, a new dissident genre with its roots in Kentucky and Bill Monroe. During the Great Depression of the 1930s, he rewrote the rules of folk, bringing in mournful rural blues and the limping sway of boogie woogie. With his band, the Blue Grass Boys, a melting pot of talented musicians including Lester Flatt and Earl Scruggs, he recorded *Blue Moon of Kentucky*, which was later covered by Elvis Presley. It was a glowing tribute to the state of Kentucky, where rumour has it that the sun setting over the prairie grasses produces shimmering blue reflections, giving rise to the term bluegrass, which won over new fans at the beginning of the 21st century thanks to the film, *O Brother, Where Art Thou?* Sadly Bill Monroe died in 1996 before he could see his music triumph with the adventures of the Soggy Bottom Boys...

Gibson L-5 and L-5 CES

Gibson

The original Gibson L-5, the precursor of the modern guitar, emerged from the Kalamazoo factory with sound engineer and luthier Lloyd Loar's signature, in 1922. The new instrument of the people was born. Although it was still acoustic, the L-5 Professional Special Grand Concert model was developed to rival the sound produced by banjos and brass instruments in jazz orchestras.

At the request of musicians, whose playing evolved as guitars improved, the L-5 was given a cutaway in 1935. The addition meant that soloists could reach the high notes more easily. But without any amplification, the notes at the bottom of the neck were sometimes hard to hear, but it wasn't until 1951 that Gibson gave its famous Archtop L-5 model a pickup. With its indent for solos and magnetic pickup, the L-5 CES (*Cutaway Electric Spanish*) combined the comfort and resonance of an acoustic guitar with the modern feel of an electric guitar.

It played a crucial role in the musical life of the 20th century. It could be seen in the hands of jazz greats such as Eddie Lang and Wes Montgomery, as well as of country giants like the Carter Family and Scotty Moore, as well as Elvis Presley, bridging the gap to rock 'n' roll.

Gibson L-5 (1934), Carter Family (without cut-away).

Gibson L-5 CES Tal Farlow.

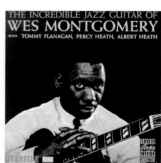

DEFINITIVE TRACKS

Keep on the Sunny Side	**Carter Family**
Wildwood Flower	**Carter Family**
West Coast Blues	**Wes Montgomery**
Mr. Walker	**Wes Montgomery**

Guitar Heroes

Maybelle Carter grew up playing hillbilly music in the hills of her native Virginia, with her cousin Sara who went on to marry amateur singer, Alvin Carter, in 1915. Maybelle married Ezra, Alvin's brother. And so the Carter Family was born. They toured the Deep South in the 1920s playing traditional songs which would become hits across America.

When success came, Maybelle spent all her savings on the most beautiful archtop guitar available, the luxurious L-5 1928 model, for $150. A sturdy guitar that kept going throughout the Carter Family's 50-year career. Maybelle played it with gusto, and her very own style, attacking melodies on the bass strings with her thumb and rhythmically strumming the high notes with her fingers. Johnny Cash who married her daughter, June Carter, credited her with inventing country music. The L-5 that belonged to Mother Maybelle, considered to be at the very heart of country music, can be seen at the Nashville Country Music Hall of Fame.

Wes Montgomery, played nothing but a custom L-5 CES with a rounded Florentine cutaway, throughout his career. After hearing Charlie Christian playing an electric guitar when he was 19, he bought his first *jazz box*, as he referred to it, for $350. Playing the guitar was nothing but a way for him to help make ends meet. He married young and soon had a family to feed. During the day, he worked in a factory, and in the evenings, he did the rounds of the jazz clubs with his two brothers Monk and Buddy.

To learn how to play his L-5 without plugging it into an amp or disturbing his family, Montgomery developed a unique playing technique, using his right thumb for the downstrokes, creating a muffled sound, and his left hand for octaves (the same note on two different strings), creating a revolutionary harmonic richness.

A self-taught musician, he went on to become one of the most influential guitarists of modern music. Just listen to "The Incredible Jazz Guitar of Wes Montgomery": all of the magic of his inimitable style is there. Stunning!

This master of the six-string guitar passed away in 1968 aged 45, no doubt exhausted by the frenzied rhythm of his short but intense existence. Disciples of the smooth jazz school have kept his spirit alive, led by the likes of Tuck Andress, Pat Metheny and George Benson.

Gibson L-5 CES Wes Montgomery.

TRADE SECRETS

The L-5 is a top-of-the-range guitar from Gibson's Master Model catalogue. The rare woods are carefully chosen to offer flawless tuning. The acoustics are naturally amplified by the sound box which is carved from a single piece of solid wood, and punctuated for the first time with f-holes, as more commonly seen on violins. Its power is boosted by its floating bridge which is held in place by the tension in the strings, distributing energy as efficiently as possible. The neck, which has to remain straight and cannot be distorted by the tension of the strings, is fitted with a truss rod — a strip of metal slipped inside the wood to control its flexibility. This was invented by Thaddeus McHugh, one of Orville Gibson's first colleagues, and is still used today. In the early 1950s, amplification for the L-5 was provided by a single Alnico P-90. In 1957, it was fitted with twin humbuckers, at the request of Wes Montgomery.

The curved cutaway near the neck is described as Venetian (as opposed to a pointed one, or Florentine). Both have been used at different times on the L-5.

Gibson J-200

Gibson J-200.

The J-200 is the ultimate acoustic country and western guitar. Nicknamed the "king of the flat tops", it has been the intimate companion of a long list of singer-songwriters ever since it was first made in 1937 for the "Singing Cowboy" Ray Whitley. The Super Jumbo, with its generous shape and meticulous finish, was immediately adopted by Gene Autry and Roy Rodgers, key figures in Hollywood Westerns, who were keen to personalise their models.

It first appeared in 1939 as the Super Jumbo 200, because of its size... and its price: $200. The finish was sunburst, like all the early Gibsons, to mask flaws in the wood. It was only after the war, in 1947, that the blonde version was baptised the J-200, with its polished spruce sound board.

In the 1960s, it was played by Elvis Presley and Bob Dylan (on his "Nashville Skyline" album, most notably on the famous duet with Johnny Cash, *Girl from the North Country*). You'd be forgiven for losing count of famous fans of the J-200 today – from Oasis' Noel Gallagher to Sheryl Crow, proudly brandishing the model on stage and in their videos.

Gibson J-200 signature Pete Townshend.

DEFINITIVE TRACKS

Love Hurts	Emmylou Harris (with Gram Parsons)
Wayfaring Stranger	Emmylou Harris
Let it Be Me	The Everly Brothers
Bye Bye Love	The Everly Brothers
Pinball Wizard	The Who
Won't Get Fooled Again	The Who

Guitar Heroes

It isn't just singing cowboys who use the J-200 – it's also popular with famous cowgirl **Emmylou Harris**! When she was still a student, she learnt her craft on a J-50 with folk tunes by Bob Dylan and Joan Baez. In the 1970s, she fell for the charms of Gram Parsons, one of country rock's most influential guitarists. Their duet launched her singing career. In 1974, she released her first album, "Pieces of Sky", accompanied by musicians who had played with Elvis Presley, which proved to be a hit with mainstream audiences.

She became one of the most famous female faces of country music, alongside Dolly Parton and Linda Rondstadt with whom she regularly records trios.

The J-200 is her favourite guitar; she has two of them, one black, decorated with roses (as seen on the album "Blue Kentucky Girl"), the other painted pink (for "The Ballad of Sally Rose", a tribute album to her musical partner Gram Parsons, who had died of an overdose). Since 2002, Emmylou Harris has had her very own signature model, the L-200, produced along the same lines as the J-200 but on a smaller scale.

The amplification system is the same as for the J-200, which, according to Emmylou Harris, is one of the jewels of American culture.

The J-200 entered into pop legend thanks to *Tommy*, the rock opera by The Who. Guitarist **Pete Townshend** wrote *Pinball Wizard* on an acoustic guitar with a pulsating rhythm that was revolutionary back in 1968. The magic continued with *Won't Get Fooled Again*, still using the same guitar, a truly gut-wrenching song. Pete isn't the type to get sentimental about his instruments. For him, they're just chunks of wood that he usually ends up smashing on stage…

But his Super Jumbo 200 managed to escape this fate, and can now live out a peaceful existence behind the window of the Rock 'n' Roll Hall of Fame Museum in Cleveland. Since February 2004, Pete Townshend has owned a model of the J-200 blessed with his own name, signed with his own hand on the end of the neck.

The most famous harmonising duo of the 1950s, the **Everly Brothers**, were great fans of the J-200. Don and Phil's voices blended perfectly as they strummed out chords on their big Western Gibsons, keeping close to their country roots. They would often personalise their guitars with double pickguards. Gibson created the signature flat top Everly Brothers model in 1962, with the famous pickguard covering almost the whole of the body. It's not that special to look at, but this feature reduces resonance that gets in the way of harmony singing. And given the number of hits they had, it must work! The masters of harmonies influenced greats from The Beatles to Simon & Garfunkel, not forgetting The Byrds. Neil Young introduced them when they were inducted into the Rock 'n' Roll Hall of Fame in 1986, pointing out that every musical group he belonged to had tried to copy the Everly Brothers' harmonies…

TRADE SECRETS

The Jumbo is a flat top guitar inspired by the hefty Gibson Super 400 with its rounded body. It has the same opulent shape, giving it unrivalled power. The sides, back and neck are maple while the top is solid sitka, a very hard wood from North America giving it a rich, crystal clear sound which can handle a certain level of forcefulness, which contributes to its popularity among country rock musicians.

The J-200 stands out from all other acoustic guitars thanks to its rosewood moustache bridge with its mother-of-pearl inlays. The other recognisable part of the Jumbo is the faux tortoiseshell pickguard, engraved with floral patterns.

Now, all of Gibson's new acoustic guitars are made in the Bozeman centre in Montana, including an excellent and more affordable Jumbo, made of mahogany and lacking in any ornamentation: the J-100.

© Knips /DALLE

Gibson ES-150

The ES-150 was the first jazz guitar with a pickup. When it was created in 1936, Gibson already had 40 years of experience producing acoustic instruments. So it was high time that they started amplifying them to make sure they could be clearly heard from the midst of big bands that were growing bigger and bigger. The first attempts used lap steels – Hawaiian guitars – played flat. That was what gave the HE-150 amp its name (Hawaiian Electric), sold with the ES-150 (Electric Spanish) for the modest price of $150.

The result was quite astounding: the electric guitar rhythms were a match for the orchestra, and solos could easily compete with the brass section.

Towards the end of the 1930s, the first jazz guitarist to use it was Eddie Durham. He introduced the magic of the electric guitar to Charlie Christian, who made the guitar a highly respected jazz instrument. His name will always be associated with the Gibson ES-150.

DEFINITIVE TRACKS

Call it Stormy Monday	T-Bone Walker
T-Bone Blues	T-Bone Walker
Swing to Bop (Topsy)	Charlie Christian
	(1941 – live at Minton's – jam sessions)
Solo Flight	Charlie Christian
	(Benny Goodman and his Orchestra)

Guitar Heroes

The grand master of the ES-150, **Charlie Christian**, brought the guitar to the forefront of the jazz scene. Born in Texas in 1916, he started playing as a very young boy, accompanying his father, busking on the street with guitars made from cigar boxes. When he was 15, he was picked to play in a big band, and there he discovered the ES-150 and its amp.

Producer John Hammond recommended him to Benny Goodman. Initially sceptical, the clarinettist and bandleader invited him to join his group in 1939 after a rather impressive half-hour improvisation. To really appreciate his creative freedom and the links that Charlie Christian forged between swing and bebop, you have to listen to the jam sessions at Minton's. It was customary at the New York club to bring together musicians looking for new trends. With the likes of Charlie Christian, Thelonious Monk, Dizzy Gillespie and Charlie Parker, bebop was born.

With his ES-150, the first virtuoso of the electric guitar was also the first to be sacrificed for his art. He died of tuberculosis at the tender age of 26, having neglected his health in the maelstrom of tours and sleepless nights.

Blues maestro, **T-Bone Walker** was never without his electric guitar. He acquired a taste for performing when he accompanied Cab Calloway as a member of his big band. With his Gibson secured with a shoulder-strap over impeccable outfits, T-Bone Walker danced and sang, a true performer, with impressive stunts including doing the splits while playing his guitar behind his back.

Such tricks inspired the likes of Chuck Berry and of course Jimi Hendrix, who admitted to imitating him as a child. In 1936, he was one of the first men to pick up an ES-150 to play the blues. He incorporated jazz chords, and separated each note by pulling on the strings. And so "bending" was born. B. B. King started playing the electric guitar after hearing T-Bone Walker's classic *Call it Stormy Monday*.

A world away from the down-at-heel misery of the blues, he created an upbeat style which was truly his own: he is regarded as an inspiration for rhythm and blues and soul music. T-Bone Walker continued to perform until the 1970s before he died of pneumonia in 1975.

Charlie Christian,
c. 1940.

TRADE SECRETS

To produce its first electric acoustic guitar, Gibson kept the risk factor to a minimum by giving a cheap L-50 guitar a pickup on the neck with two potentiometers. This prototype pickup, developed by musical inventor Alvino Rey, was worked on by Walter Fuller, an engineer at Gibson, before the product could go on sale. The magnetic pickup consisted of large magnets made of an alloy of aluminium, nickel and cobalt, surrounded by an electric wire coil. This produces a magnetic field which reacts to the vibrations of the steel strings.

Its width, encompassing all of the strings in its magnetic field, gives it the reputation today among some jazz musicians of being the best pickup of all time. Apart from its bulk, the disadvantage is that it picks up all the annoying noises from the immediate vicinity, giving rise to some rather amusing situations. Gibson managed to reduce the danger by going on to invent the P-90 and the humbucker.

Gibson Super 400

In 1934, Gibson took a gamble on the rise of the guitar and produced a larger, more luxurious model costing $400: the aptly named Super 400. A real extravagance at a time when America was only just starting to emerge from the Great Depression. In the first year, just 63 guitars were ordered from the Kalamazoo factory, and a measly 23 the year after that. A rather discouraging start, but it does mean that these early editions are now highly prized – and highly priced – collectors' pieces.

But Gibson didn't lose heart and continued to believe in the power of the Super 400. In 1937, it was redesigned with a rounded Venetian cutaway so that jazz guitarists could access the high notes at the top of the neck more easily. With a more demure, but also more dynamic line, it could easily make itself heard in a hillbilly orchestra or Western swing band. Fitted with pickups, the Super 400 is ready with a more robust sound to keep up with the new vigour of rockabilly, in preparation for the advent of rock 'n' roll in the early 1950s.

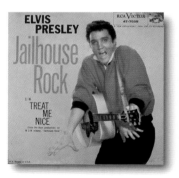

DEFINITIVE TRACKS

Jailhouse Rock	Scotty Moore
Big Hunk O'Love	Scotty Moore
Smoke Smoke Smoke That Cigarette	Merle Travis
Sixteen Tons	Merle Travis

Guitar Heroes

© GAB Archives-Redferns/DALLE

Born on 27th December 1931 in Tennessee, **Scotty Moore** is a legendary guitarist, the King's right-hand man in the Pantheon of rock 'n' roll! He was already under contract with Sun Records in Memphis when Sam Phillips suggested him as an accompanist for a young Elvis Presley at his first recording on 5th July 1954. That night, accompanied by double bass player Bill Black (with whom Scotty went on to form the Blue Moon Boys), Presley and Moore recorded *That's All Right*, regarded as pretty much the first example of rock 'n' roll. The rest is history! The main characteristic of the playing style is the way an electric guitar is made to sound very natural, first with the ES-295, then with the L-5. Scotty Moore got hold of his first Super 400 in 1957 after signing an endorsement contract with Gibson when he was recording the soundtrack for the film *Jailhouse Rock*. He never looked back, continuing to use this comfortable yet powerful guitar for the rest of his career. "The Guitar that Changed the World", as the title of one of his solo albums announced in the 1960s, when Elvis had set off for Hollywood. Equipped with a spangly Super 400, Scotty came back to the stage alongside the King for American TV's famous *NBC Special*.

For his comeback in the 1990s, he got hold of a new Super 400 Gibson to play with All The King's Men, a super group made up of the likes of Jeff Beck and Keith Richards.

When you look at **Merle Travis'** special Super 400, you might think that its flashy decoration was quite the thing in the 1930s. The name of that smiling pioneer from Kentucky is emblazoned across the neck, and the headstock is covered with ornaments that are perfectly coordinated with his trademark cowboy outfit. Putting these aesthetic details to one side, Merle Travis is nothing less than a genius who created the country music style with his finger-picking technique: picking out the rhythm on the bass strings with his thumb while the melody is played on the high strings. His most loyal disciples include luminaries such as Chet Atkins, Scotty Moore and Carl Perkins. The talented musician also wrote countless hits including *Smoke Smoke Smoke That Cigarette*, which was even covered in France by Eddy Mitchell in the smoke-filled 1960s. Merle Travis could turn his hand to anything – he even designed a prototype guitar which helped Leo Fender produce his first Solid Body Electric guitar in 1948. His Super 400 is rightly on show at the Country Music Hall of Fame in Nashville.

TRADE SECRETS

The first ever models bore the inscription "L-5 Deluxe", describing the generous size of the instrument. It's a guitar with a traditionally sculpted sound board combined with the Super Grand Auditorium Size, more commonly called the Super 400. The largest guitar body produced by Gibson is carved from a single piece of solid wood, cut in two then joined in the middle to retain the symmetry of the grain of the wood. Admirable craftsmanship on the little mechanical pieces, painstakingly decorated, as well as on the tuner knobs, each one engraved in a graceful floral pattern. Even the floating pickguard, intended to protect the sound board from the pick, is decorated with ornate mother-of-pearl inlay. An art deco jewel. Nothing was too good for this deluxe guitar, explaining its extravagant price. The Super 400 is easily recognisable from its Y-shaped tailpiece, engraved with its name, and the logo in the shape of a divided diamond that would later be used on Custom models. In 1951 the Super 400 CES (*Cutaway Electric Spanish*) appeared with two P-90 pickups, a first for Gibson, with separate tone and volume controls. As of 1957, it proudly came with humbucker pickups.

Gibson J-45

The warm, dusky sound of the acoustic J-45 can be heard on countless recordings of country, folk and blues music. This demure but fascinating guitar is now firmly ensconced in the history of music. One of its most famous players is Bob Dylan, who recorded his first three acoustic albums with a J-50 (natural wood finish), the perfect accompaniment to singers, with bass notes that are rounded without being overwhelming. It has also been used by great blues guitarist Lightnin' Hopkins, who was famous for his picking technique, playing with a folky twist. Bruce Springsteen liked to use his precious vintage J-45 vintage for his studio recordings.

The J-45 came on to the market in 1942, at a time when the world was in turmoil, as a cheaper alternative to the Jumbo range. It was a very good guitar, which was also affordable, costing just $45, making it one of the most popular acoustic guitars of the folk era, played by the pioneers of the protest song, Woody Guthrie and Peter Seeger. The first models had a little gold banner across the headstock saying: *"Only a Gibson is good enough."* The J-45 hasn't changed that much since then, and is still produced in Gibson's workshops in Montana.

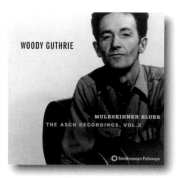

DEFINITIVE TRACKS

The Wizard of Strings	Roy Smeck
Tip-Toe Thru' the Tulips with Me	Nick Lucas
Mr. Tambourine Man	Bob Dylan
Subterranean Homesick Blues	Bob Dylan
This Land Is Your Land	Woody Guthrie

Guitar Heroes

Gibson launched its first flat-top acoustic model in 1928, with the **Nick Lucas** guitar. A very manageable model, suitable for the stage and radio recordings, which made him the first artist to associate his name with an instrument. Nicknamed the Crooning Troubadour, with his little guitar over his shoulder, he won over audiences on the stage in Broadway. In 1929, his hit record *Tip-Toe Through the Tulips* made number one, and his long career as a jazz guitarist and crooner helped popularise Gibson's flat-top guitars. In the 1960s, Bob Dylan used an exact replica of the little Nick Lucas Special to record his album "Bringing it All Back Home"; it was immortalised in the documentary that was made by D. A. Pennebaker of the UK tour in 1965, released as *Don't Look Back*.

Roy Smeck was the second big name to become associated with a guitar. Smeck was a genius with any stringed instrument you care to mention: banjo, ukulele, Spanish guitar... He allegedly recorded more than 500 78s for various companies; he even took part in the first musical film for Vitaphone, the ancestor of the music video, launched by Warner Bros. His name appeared on a Gibson in 1930: the Roy Smeck Stage Deluxe Guitar. A Jumbo model with a corresponding jumbo sound. The man they called The Wizard of Strings died aged 94, renowned for his expertise on the ukulele.

The J-45 was used as a template for **Woody Guthrie's** famous Southern Jumbo. This guitar was seen as a secret weapon by this early protest singer. He wrote the famous slogan on his guitar case: "*This machine kills fascists*". During the Great Depression, the hero of American folk was the incarnation of the mythical singing vagabond, telling stories of the people, for the people, singing songs about social conflict, paving the way for the folk revival of the 1960s, most notably for Bob Dylan, who dedicated his first composition to him in his hospital bed: *Song to Woody*. Woody Guthrie said that he wrote a song a day before he became paralysed by Huntingdon's disease. One of his most famous hits, *This Land Is Your Land*, is widely regarded as America's alternative national anthem, a concert staple for Bruce Springsteen.

Woody Guthrie.

© GEMS-Redferns/DALLE

TRADE SECRETS

The J-45 is part of the Jumbo series, characterised by its powerful sound projection. Its shape is along the same lines as the Dreadnought, invented by Martin. Under the spruce top, the x-bracing is adjusted to cope with the tension of the strings without inhibiting the vibration of the sound box. The solid mahogany back and the sides produce clear, but not brilliant, high notes. The teardrop-shaped pickguard is attached right next to the sound hole, protecting the guitar from the pick of more vigorous folk singers. The rounded mahogany neck is nicknamed the "baseball bat" because of its comfort and the way it fits the hand. Like all Gibsons from the era, the sunburst finish is intended to hide flaws in the wood, which was hard to come by in times of worldwide conflict.

Its dark brown shaded colour remains the J-45's trademark. The J-50 was the model with a natural wood finish that came out after the war. A huge number of J-45s were produced and so they are not particularly sought-after by collectors, but that doesn't take anything away from their quality. The price of an original model is still very affordable for such a legendary guitar.

Gibson ES-335

With its deep, velvety sound – perfect for the blues – and its striking punch – ideal for rock 'n' roll – it is one of Gibson's most mythical guitars. Its best advertisement is a brilliant radio clip with a young country boy who plays the guitar just like ringing a bell. Of course it's none other than *Johnny B. Goode*, the almost autobiographical story of its writer, Chuck Berry.

To appreciate the sound produced by an ES-335, just listen to the intros to the former beautician's classic hits (*Rock and Roll Music, Maybellene, You Never Can Tell, Roll Over Beethoven* to name but a few). Stunning creativity and a matchless contribution to the history of rock, leading John Lennon to say "If you tried to give rock and roll another name, you might call it Chuck Berry."

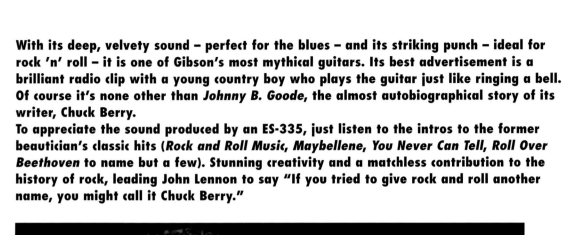

Gibson
ES-335 Cherry.

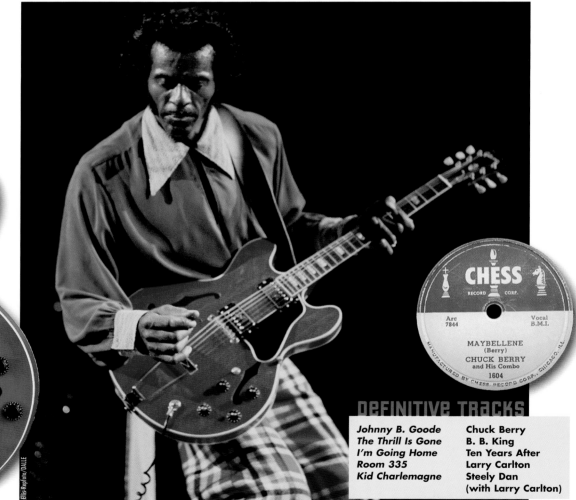

CHESS
RECORD CORP.
Arc
7844
Vocal
B.M.I.
MAYBELLENE
(Berry)
CHUCK BERRY
and His Combo
1604
MANUFACTURED BY CHESS RECORD CORP., CHICAGO, ILL.

© Ellis-Repfoto/DALLE

DEFINITIVE TRACKS

Johnny B. Goode	Chuck Berry
The Thrill Is Gone	B. B. King
I'm Going Home	Ten Years After
Room 335	Larry Carlton
Kid Charlemagne	Steely Dan
	(with Larry Carlton)

Guitar Heroes

As well as Chuck Berry, the ES-335 is associated with the work and the image of a number of rock and blues giants. **B. B. King**, a keen ambassador of the ES-335, is a pioneer of blues music. In 2005, at the age of 80, he embarked on a world tour which lasted until 2007. *Rolling Stone* magazine ranked him in the top five greatest guitarists of all time. His ES-335, affectionately nicknamed Lucille, played a key role in his career. B. B. King even wrote one of his most famous songs to extol its virtues: a scuffle broke out in a club over a woman called Lucille. The scuffle led to a fire, and King risked his life to save his guitar from the flames. Guitarist and guitar have been inseparable ever since, and King treats Lucille with the utmost respect. So he never sings and plays at the same time – after all, it's rude to interrupt a lady! Just listen to the dialogue between the voice and the guitar on *The Thrill Is Gone* which won him his first Grammy Award. Since 1981, the Lucille has been one of Gibson's signature models. To comply with B. B. King's demands, it's fitted with a varitone and a stereo output, and its name appears in mother-of-pearl along the neck.

Alvin Lee, guitarist with Ten Years After, propelled the ES-335 into the modern world, crashing through fretboard speed records with his famous solo in *I'm Going Home* at Woodstock in 1969. Budding guitar heroes always have a stab at reproducing his guitar skills as heard on his Big Red, which is now estimated to be worth somewhere in the region of $500,000. For his tours, he had replicas (transfers and all) made by Gibson Custom Shop to sell to the general public. Not bad for a guitar bought for $90 when he was starting out at 16!

Mr. 335 himself, according to fans and the music press thanks to his famous instrumental *Room 335,* studio guitarist **Larry Carlton** produces a sweet, smooth sound on his Gibson. He even went so far as to nickname his personal recording studio "Room 335". Then of course there's "Mr. 335 Live in Japan" and "The Best of Mr. 335". It's as if the guitar is a part of his body. In the 1970s, at the height of his career, his name appeared on the sleeves of over 500 albums. He recorded with true greats including Michael Jackson, Quincy Jones, Diana Ross, Joni Mitchell and jazz-rock fusion band Steely Dan, for whom he came up with the solo for *Kid Charlemagne*, voted one of the three best guitar songs of all time by *Rolling Stone* magazine.

TRADE SECRETS

To keep up with evolutions in this new style of music, the ES-335 makes the most of all the new techniques thought up by Gibson's engineers. The solid block running through the centre, thought up by Les Paul for the first electric guitars, is the mainstay. It improves sustain, making notes last as long as possible. But to keep the feel of an acoustic guitar, the designers surrounded it with a thinner archtop to reduce feedback at loud volumes. Its classic shape, with a large curved body decorated with two f-holes, reminiscent of Spanish guitars, hence the initials ES – again for Electric Spanish – and 335 for its price in dollars when it came out in 1958! So that players could reach the high notes right at the top of the neck, the body has a curved Venetian cutaway. The last trade secret is that it's fitted with dual-coil humbucker pickups which avoid lags in the signal and give it a warmer, less metallic sound. The only disadvantage is that it is a large guitar and quite heavy, so be careful with those shoulders. You need quite a wide strap if you want to emulate Check Berry and cross the stage doing his famous duck walk…

Gibson Les Paul Gold Top

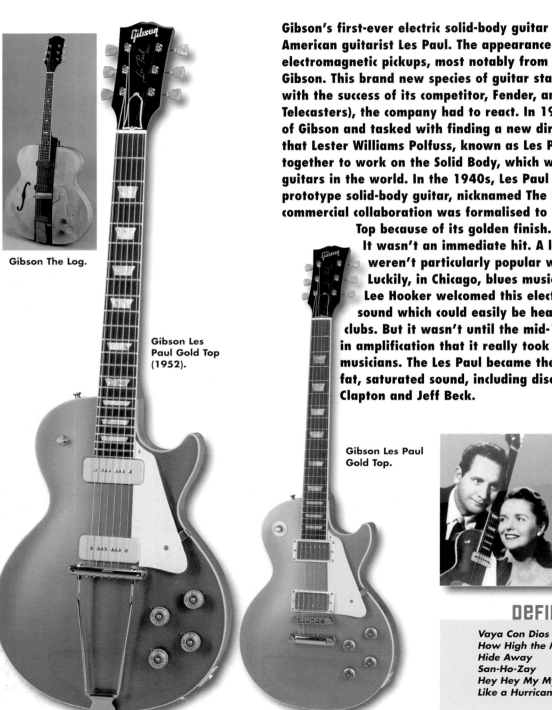

Gibson's first-ever electric solid-body guitar was given the name of its designer, American guitarist Les Paul. The appearance of solid-body guitars fitted with electromagnetic pickups, most notably from Fender, presented a new challenge for Gibson. This brand new species of guitar started to create quite a buzz, especially with the success of its competitor, Fender, and their Broadcasters (later becoming Telecasters), the company had to react. In 1950, Ted McCarty was chosen as President of Gibson and tasked with finding a new direction for the company; he recommended that Lester Williams Polfuss, known as Les Paul, to put his name and his expertise together to work on the Solid Body, which went on to become one of the most famous guitars in the world. In the 1940s, Les Paul had actually already experimented with a prototype solid-body guitar, nicknamed The Log, which Gibson had rejected. In 1952, a commercial collaboration was formalised to bring out the first Les Paul, called the Gold Top because of its golden finish.

It wasn't an immediate hit. A lot of the innovative features of the model weren't particularly popular with more conservative jazz guitarists. Luckily, in Chicago, blues musicians such as Muddy Waters and John Lee Hooker welcomed this electric guitar with its rich, decidedly modern sound which could easily be heard in the hustle and bustle of the blues clubs. But it wasn't until the mid-1960s and the technical advances made in amplification that it really took off, highly sought-after by British blues musicians. The Les Paul became the perfect six-string guitar for fans of its fat, saturated sound, including disciples of the likes of Jimmy Page, Eric Clapton and Jeff Beck.

Gibson The Log.

Gibson Les Paul Gold Top (1952).

Gibson Les Paul Gold Top.

DEFINITIVE TRACKS

Vaya Con Dios	Les Paul & Mary Ford
How High the Moon	Les Paul & Mary Ford
Hide Away	Freddie King
San-Ho-Zay	Freddie King
Hey Hey My My	Neil Young
Like a Hurricane	Neil Young

Guitar Heroes

In 1952, **Les Paul** was already a well-known guitarist, sharing a stage with the likes of Django Reinhardt, Nat King Cole and Bing Crosby. He wasn't just an inventive designer; he was a very popular musician. That was one of the reasons why Gibson asked him to launch the guitar that made rock 'n' roll possible.

Lester William Polfuss was born in Wisconsin in 1915 and acquired a love of the guitar at an early age listening to Eddie Lang, jazz's first great electric guitarist. In 1948, his right arm was shattered in a car accident. He asked the surgeon to set his arm at a guitar-playing angle, so that only his wrist could move. He had a larger than normal plectrum made so that he could hold it more easily. As well as inventing the guitar that would revolutionise modern music, Les Paul enjoyed great success in the 1950s as a musician, both as a soloist and as part of a duo with his wife Mary Ford. Something else we owe this brilliant mind is the first ever example of multitrack recordings. After years spent focusing on his business, he picked up his guitar again and in 1977, won a Grammy Award for his album "Chester and Lester", with Chet Atkins. As we write, Les Paul is still jamming on a regular basis at his favourite New York club, The Iridium Jazz Club, where many a guitarist goes to pay tribute to him.

In 1954, **Freddy** (or **Freddie**) **King** was one of the first blues guitarists to play on a Gold Top. King's husky low notes and funky rhythms, with his picking solos using his thumb and his index finger, influenced a whole generation of young white guitarists including Peter Green, Mick Taylor, Eric Clapton… basically, every hero of the 1960s British Blues Boom you care to think of.

He is one of the guitarists most highly admired by Clapton, who covered *Hide Away* on his first album with John Mayall & The Bluesbreakers in 1966. In the 1970s, he invited Freddie King to join him on tour. A gifted poker player, King seized the opportunity to fleece Clapton for up to $2,000 a night… With no hard feelings, Clapton produced King's last album, "Burglar", which came out in 1974. King didn't get much of a chance to enjoy this recognition: he died of a heart attack 18 months later.

Neil Young's Old Black

Since 1969, Neil Young's favoured guitar, which he takes everywhere with him, is an Old Black 1953 Gold Top fitted with a Bigsby pickup. The stunning sound of this guitar is down to the fact that Neil Young swapped the original P-90 pickup, which wasn't powerful enough, for a mini-humbucker from a Firebird. And to control his ear-splitting outbursts, he has his very own special piece of kit, the Whizzer, which physically changes his 1959 Fender Deluxe amplifier's settings on demand, without him having to do anything manually. Magic! Neil Young is a keen guitar collector and likes to buy them second hand, then write a song or two. Once that's happened he puts them away in a corner and goes back to his Old Black.

Trade Secrets

Les Paul baptised it Gold Top, not just for its golden finish, which was meant to protect its trade secrets, but also to reiterate the excellent quality of this guitar which combines tradition and innovation. The slightly rounded shape of the Les Paul, is directly inspired by traditional Gibsons, quite simply because the tools used to make them were already available in the factory in Kalamazoo! It's slightly smaller than its big sisters, with a cutaway to improve access to the high notes. But the main feature of the Les Paul is its tonality, produced by the use of two wood species: flame maple for the top, which had been used for violins before then, and mahogany for the body, giving it excellent stability to sustain the notes.

Opinion is divided as to Les Paul's actual involvement in the design. He claims to have come up with look of the body of the guitar, and suggested the idea of the two pickups, a single coil P-90 near the bridge for the high notes, and an Alnico pickup for the low notes at the neck. The harmonic frequencies are actually different depending on the position of the pickup. In Ted McCarty's opinion, Les Paul's contribution finished with the trapeze-style bridge, which was soon replaced by the Tune-O-Matic. Les Paul is still the name that will always be associated with the Gold Top though. It was produced until 1958, when it became available in four different models: the Standard, the Junior, the Custom and the Special, all of which went on to become classics. There are now some one hundred different models in the catalogue.

Gibson Les Paul Custom

The Custom is the deluxe Les Paul model. It appeared in 1954, with a black finish "to look like a tuxedo", as requested by its designer Paul, who nicknamed it Black Beauty. Gibson pulled out all the stops for its demanding jazz customers, giving it golden hardware to really stand out against the dark background. But in an era of new performance styles, what really captured the imagination of virtuoso guitarists was the quality and speed of the neck, with its wide, flat frets, giving it the nickname, the Fretless Wonder. And so in 1955, the Custom was perfectly equipped to be part of the first ever rock 'n' roll record, with *Rock Around the Clock* in the hands of Frank Beecher, the lead guitarist for Bill Haley & His Comets.

Gibson
Les Paul Custom
Black Beauty.

Gibson
Les Paul Custom
Jimmy Page.

Gibson
Les Paul Custom
Steve Jones.

DEFINITIVE TRACKS

Get It On	T-Rex
20th Century Boy	T-Rex
Hot Love	T-Rex
Anarchy in the UK	Sex Pistols
God Save the Queen	Sex Pistols
Show Me the Way	Peter Frampton
Rock Around the Clock	Bill Haley & His Comets

Guitar Heroes

Marc Bolan, one of rock music's most influential characters, was a devoted fan of the Gibson Les Paul. With his band, T-Rex, he moved straight from folky sitting-on-the-floor-with-bongos music, to striking boogie rock which would bring him a great deal of success. On the sleeve of the first eponymous T-Rex album, marking the dawn of the glam rock era, he poses proudly with his wood-finish Custom 57. In 1970, Marc Bolan's rock teenager unleashed an epidemic of T-Rexmania in Great Britain. His androgynous look, with his satin, clothes, sequins and make-up, inspired bands like Sweet, Roxy Music and Slade, not to mention his friend David Bowie, who took the world by storm with Ziggy Stardust just when Bolan's star was beginning to fade. In 1977,

embraced by the punk scene, Bolan was on the brink of a comeback when he died in a car crash. The Damned and the Sex Pistols, who considered themselves heirs to Electric Warrior's legacy, plugged in their Gibsons and carried on where he had left off …

Jimmy Page, Led Zeppelin's guitarist, had a Black Beauty with a Bigsby vibrato tailpiece with three pickups, a gift from Keith Richards. But it was stolen in 1970 and never recovered.

In 1977 **Steve Jones**, guitarist with the Sex Pistols, showed off a stunning white Custom that had belonged to Sylvain Sylvain of the New York Dolls. One of the rare instruments that he didn't steal in his punk period…

Peter Frampton, golden-curled rock guitarist with Humble Pie, rocketed to international stardom with his 1976 live album "Frampton Comes Alive", thanks in part to his use of a talk box which added a human voice effect to his Custom.

Trade Secrets

This time, the whole body and the sound board are made of mahogany, a wood with a very light average density, giving it a clear, warm sound aimed at jazz guitarists. The Custom came with all the latest technological innovations developed in Gibson's workshops. The Tune-O-Matic bridge was marketed for the first time on the Custom with the blessing of the boss, Ted McCarty, who registered the patent in his name. With this chrome bridge, the settings for each string can be adjusted separately to guarantee consistency along the whole length of the string. Most manufacturers have been using it ever since. But the real revolution came in 1957, when the noisy single coil P-90 pickups were replaced with the new humbuckers, invented by Seth Lover.

Literally, it cancels out the hum to produce a round, dense, soft sound, which would make Gibson guitars so famous. One of the most famous Custom models was fitted with three PAF pickups to produce a range of sounds by multiplying the combinations with a switch. The first pickups had to wait for a few years before the patent was approved, which is why humbucker pickups are often described as PAFs (PAF stands for "Patent Applied For"). In 1968, Gibson started to reissue the Custom, now available in white, cherry red and natural wood as well as the original black model.

Gibson Les Paul Standard

Gibson Les Paul Standard 1959, sunburst finish.

The Les Paul Standard is without a doubt Gibson's most famous guitar: Jimmy Page used one throughout his career, Eric Clapton introduced it to Jeff Beck, Peter Green and Mick Taylor. With the Standard, Frank Zappa invented jazz-rock fusion, Santana made Woodstock audiences get up and dance and Slash gave hard rock a new 1980s twist with Guns N' Roses. And yet this guitar nearly didn't make it: fewer than 2,000 copies were produced between 1958 and 1960, and in 1961, it was replaced with the SG (Solid Guitar), which was better suited to counter the onslaught of Fender's Telecasters and Stratocasters.

A few years later, in the wake of the passion for blues music among the English youth, thanks to its rarity and exceptional sound quality, the Standard became a highly sought-after model. In 1968, a few came back on to the market, but it wasn't until 1975 that it was finally officially reissued. By multiplying its sound options with effects (distortion, feedback etc.) and pedals (fuzz, wah-wah) on a Marshall amp, Jimmy Page, armed with his very own Standard, would give birth to hard rock, first with the Yardbirds then with Led Zeppelin.

DEFINITIVE TRACKS

Whole Lotta Love	Led Zeppelin
Rock 'n' Roll	Led Zeppelin
All Your Love	John Mayall & The Bluesbreakers
I Feel Free	Cream
Honky Tonk Woman	Rolling Stones
Can You Hear Me Knocking	Rolling Stones

Guitar Heroes

At the age of 15, **Jimmy Page** became fascinated by a 1959 Les Paul Standard. His mother disapproved of electric guitars and wouldn't buy him one, so Jimmy bought his with money he'd earned from his holiday job. Not a bad investment if you consider all of the recordings it was used for! A popular session musician, Page played on an unbelievable number of 1960s British hits, including songs for the likes of The Kinks, The Who and Donovan, as well as French stars such as Michel Polnareff and Johnny Hallyday! But his brilliance on the guitar was first fully appreciated on an international stage with Led Zeppelin. This legendary group – with John Paul Jones, John Bonham and Robert Plant – spoke the language of the blues perfectly. From their first album, which came out in 1969, classics by Willy Dixon and Robert Johnson were given a devilish twist in the hands of Jimmy Page. When he came up with the idea of using a bow for *Dazed and Confused*, it seemed as though things had come full circle:

hadn't Orville Gibson been inspired by the legendary Stradivarius to make his guitars?

Eric Clapton bought his first Standard 1960 from Selmer when he was playing with John Mayall & The Bluesbreakers. The 21-year-old guitarist fell under the instrument's spell, impressed with its warm sound and the dense sound produced by the two humbuckers which he amplified with a Marshall amp set to max, both on stage and in the studio. The combination of the Les Paul and a Marshall produced the grandiose "Blues Breakers with Eric Clapton", also known as "The Beano album" as its cover shows Eric engrossed in a copy of the comic. His Standard, the one he considered to be his best, was stolen during rehearsals for his new group Cream's new album. Despite the hefty reward offered, he never got it back… His fans would refer to him as God – he did have a heavenly way with his guitar.

As a devoted fan of Clapton, young blues prodigy, **Mick Taylor**, had his own Les Paul. Hanging around backstage with the Bluesbreakers paid off when in 1967, he was asked to stand in for Peter Green who had left to start Fleetwood Mac. He developed his own personal bluesy style with a Standard 1959, which he bought from Keith Richards, but which was also stolen in Nellcôte (in the South of France) during the recording of the legendary "Exile on Main St". The Rolling Stones wanted Clapton to replace Brian Jones, but John Mayall recommended Mick Taylor. His first concert with the band was at Hyde Park in July 1969 in front of some half a million fans: he was an immediate hit with the crowd, fitting in with the band seamlessly until he left in 1974. You can't argue with Mick Jagger when he talks about the Mick Taylor years being the some of the Stones' best.

OH, TO BE IN ENGLAND

In 1960s Swinging London, the place to be for any musician worth his salt was Henri Selmer's shop on Charing Cross Road. It sold imported American guitars, including highly sought-after Gibsons. Rock fans and stars alike rubbed shoulders in this little store where some

members of staff went on to become famous themselves, like John McLaughlin and Paul Kossoff (later a member of Free), who clearly

remembered the day when Jimi Hendrix came to try out the guitars, playing *Little Wing* in front of the customers. Revolutionary!

TRADE SECRETS

In 1958, Gibson got back in touch with tradition, rediscovering the reassuring nature of wood. So he replaced the gold of the Gold Top, thought by some to be too garish, with a translucent finish. At last, you could see the grain of the flame maple in the orangey wood. The secret of the Standard's natural sound lies in the quality of the carefully selected wood. There isn't much difference between its structure and the Gold Top apart

from the two humbuckers that produce a more powerful, sustained sound. It has a switch on top of the sound board: rhythm for the low notes; treble for the high notes; medium for both. So, in keeping with Les Paul's fundamental principle, the guitar is totally and utterly in the hands of its player, who can control the volume, the tone and the sound of the guitar without going anywhere near the amp!

Logically, the rocketing demand caused a huge increase in the cost of original models and today, genuine Les Paul Standards from 1958–1960 – which seem to have the best dual-coil pickups ever made – are more likely to be found in the safety of a collector's display cabinet than in a musician's guitar case!

Gibson SG

Marketed as a Les Paul in 1961, with its saturated sound, this is the first electric guitar specifically designed to play rock music. It is the epitome of modernity, with its revolutionary design and a lightness which made it a must-have both for the flamboyant solos of Angus Young (AC/DC) and for the spectacular performances of Pete Townshend (The Who). The SG was involved in all the big musical trends of the 1960s, from Cream's psychedelia to the birth of heavy metal with the likes of Black Sabbath. Les Paul didn't like the shape though, finding it downright dangerous and suggesting that you could kill yourself with horns that sharp. So it was that his name was removed from the model in 1963 when his contract with Gibson came to an end. The SG is light and small, so it's perfectly suited to extravagant stage performances and ideal for spine-tingling, saturated solos... and its devilish double horns give it a suitably fiendish look.

Gibson SG signature Angus Young.

Gibson SG 61 Reissue Heritage Cherry.

DEFINITIVE TRACKS

Sunshine of Your Love	Cream
Highway to Hell	AC/DC
Paranoid	Black Sabbath
Vas-y guitare	Louis Bertignac
Stairway to Heaven	Led Zeppelin

FLOWER POWER

© Chassaing/DALLE

In 1967, **Eric Clapton** and Cream were right at the root of the Flower Power movement. Clapton had his SG painted by The Fool, a pair of Dutch artists who worked closely with The Beatles. A few months later, a bit tired of the hippie trend, he gave it to George Harrison who in turn gave it to his friend, songwriter Jackie Lomax, who sold it to American guitarist Todd Rundgren. In 2000, the SG Fool was sold as a work of art at Sotheby's in New York for $150,000.

TRADE SECRETS

The Gibson SG was designed to be comfortable for guitarists who wanted as much freedom of movement as possible on stage. The problem of weight with Solid Body was resolved by chamfering the edges of the body and the two indentations nicknamed the Devil's Horns, which were slightly asymmetrical, optimising access to the high notes. With its svelte body, two humbuckers produced a sharper, more aggressive sound, ideal for the manic energy of rock 'n' roll. The SG's ergonomic shape is crafted from a thin piece of mahogany, a light wood providing excellent sustain. The neck, attached to the body, is famed for its speed with flat frets bringing the strings even closer to the neck. In the mid-1960s, the SG became the new queen of rock and came in different models: Standard, Junior, Custom, Special and even a double neck version for Led Zeppelin's Jimmy Page.

Tony Iommi

With his group, Black Sabbath, Tony Iommi is one of the founding fathers of heavy metal. As a young metal worker in Birmingham, Tony Iommi lost the tips of two fingers on his right hand. From this twist of fate, a left-handed guitarist was born who inevitably came up with his very own personal style. He makes thimble-like prosthetics which he fits on his remaining stubs to hit the strings cleanly and sharply (metal). A bit unpleasant, but it works! To soften the chords, he loosens them a few tones which makes the sound deeper and weightier (heavy). Iommi also often uses the diminished fifth (the Tritone) or Diabolus in Musica, an interval which was frowned upon by the church until the Renaissance. Iommi's heavy, disturbing sound made a worldwide impact with *Paranoid* in 1970. Tony Iommi has his own dark-coloured signature model with cross-shaped position inlays – and somehow Beelzebub's horns look even more pointed than usual…

Angus Young

THE DOUBLE NECK – EDS 1275

Designed as two SG guitars in one – with a standard six-string neck at the bottom for rock and solo sections and a 12-string neck on top for accompanying and arpeggios – in the hands of Jimmy Page, it became a symbol of the creativity of rock in the 1970s. He first used it in 1973 to play the monumental *Stairway to Heaven* on stage without changing instrument half-way through. As well as its off-putting price (it was only made to order), its weight was enough to prevent too many tricks. In Jimmy Page's wake, a number of famous faces have had a go with the double neck, including John McLaughlin, Don Felder and Joe Walsh (the Eagles), Ace Frehley (Kiss), Alex Lifeson (Rush) and Pete Townshend (The Who). The epitome of excess for prog-rock and jazz-rock imaginations.

The best way to describe the style of Angus Young, AC/DC's fireworks chief, would be excitable. The school-uniformed hell-raiser has been inseparable from his Gibson SG since he started out in the steamy pubs and clubs of Sydney. The Young family, originally from Glasgow, set off for Australia in 1963 when Angus was just 8 years old. Every day, as soon as he got home from school, he went straight for his guitar, before he could even change out of his uniform. His older sister Margaret suggested that he keep it on when he went on stage. She was also the one who noticed the AC/DC sticker on a sewing machine. All they needed was the perfect singer to fit in with the high-voltage guitar playing of brothers Malcolm and Angus. They found him in 1974 in the shape of Bon Scott, their roadie and bodyguard. The latter passed away in 1980 after his own highway to hell, but AC/DC carried on with Brian Johnson in his unmistakable flat cap. After a career spanning 35 years and around 200 million albums worldwide, the tireless Angus Young picked up his SG once again for a new album and tour in 2008. *Let There Be Rock*!

Gibson Flying V

Gibson Flying V
Jimi Hendrix.

Gibson Flying V
(1959).

In the late 1950s, Leo Fender liked to tell everyone that Gibson was running out of ideas. President, Ted McCarty, responded by designing three daring and innovative new models: the Flying V, the Explorer and the Moderne (which never made it off the drawing board). This modernist series took its inspiration from science fiction, the space race and comics, which enjoyed cult status in the 1950s.

It was 1958 though, and guitar players weren't quite ready for these ultramodern models. It was a total failure: in the first year, a measly one hundred or so models of the Flying V were sold, and not even that many of the Explorer. The modern range was withdrawn from Gibson's catalogue.

In the late 1960s, young psychedelic blues guitarists looking for genuine Gibsons made the company reissue the Flaying V model, which was an immediate hit with Jimi Hendrix, Pete Townshend and Dave Davies (The Kinks).

DEFINITIVE TRACKS

Red House	Jimi Hendrix
Power Blues	Albert King
The First Time I Met the Blues	Albert King
Roadhouse Blues	Les Doors
Memphis	Lonnie Mack

Guitar Heroes

The Flying V became famous in the hands of blues guitarist **Albert King**, who nicknamed his Lucy. This giant was born in Mississippi, and made a name for himself with his recordings for the Stax label, in which he was accompanied by the house band Booker T. & the MGs in the 1960s. He was one of the pioneers of blues and soul fusion and contributed to the miraculous Memphis soul sound. Right in the heart of the psychedelic movement, Albert King was the first genuine blues musician to play in front of a rock audience at the Fillmore West, San Francisco's famous music venue. It was no coincidence that Jimi Hendrix adopted the Flying V after sharing the bill with the creator of *Blues Power* and *Born under a Bad Sign*…

His greatest hits have been covered and given greater airplay by the likes of Buddy Guy, Eric Clapton and Stevie Ray Vaughan, all fans of his crystal-clear solos and impressive mastery of the strings. For his 65th birthday, Billy Gibbons, guitarist with ZZ Top, gave him his very own personalised Flying V with his name engraved on the neck – a unique model produced in Nashville by Tom Holmes, the favourite luthier of the famous beards and maker of Bo Diddley's square guitars.

Jimi Hendrix used a cherry-coloured Flying V repainted in psychedelic style. It would be impossible to go unnoticed with a guitar like this; it was no doubt because of its telegenic qualities that he used it to record the legendary French programme *Dim Dam Dom* in October 1967. Towards the end of his career, as though looking for new inspiration, he stopped using his Fender Stratocasters quite so much. During his final "Cry of Love" tour, named after the album that he'd just finished, he played a black Flying V a lot. This was what he was playing on stage at the Isle of Wight festival in August 1970 in a poignant rendition of *Red House*. Estimated to be worth around $275,000, his Flying V holds court at the Hard Rock Cafe on Old Park Lane, in London.

Another big fan of the Flying V is **Lonnie Mack**, almost as famous for his country style imbued with blues as for his cowboy hat and one of the most influential characters of American rock. Lonnie Mack was born in Indiana in 1941 and left school early to start hanging out in country music clubs. As a teenager, he was one of the first to buy a Flying V in 1958. It was marked with the number 7, and he still has it today. Armed with this guitar, his reputation grew in the rock 'n'

Lonnie Mack.

roll world as a session guitarist and he recorded with the likes of Freddy King and James Brown.

In 1968, he signed with Elektra, which was The Doors' label too. He played the solo on *Roadhouse Blues* from the album "Morrison Hotel". He recorded his own albums at the same time as working as artistic director for the same label. He also discovered the talented Stevie Ray Vaughan; together they went on to record "Strike Like Lightning". Highly esteemed by his peers, Lonnie Mack frequently appeared on stage with his Flying V number 7 to jam with the likes of Keith Richards, Ron Wood and Ry Cooder.

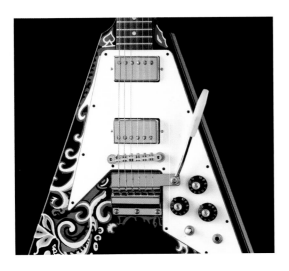

TRADE SECRETS

With its avant-garde straight lines, the Flying V broke with the traditional image of Gibson's curved guitars, inspired by automotive and aeronautical designs. The body was originally made of afara – a light wood with unique acoustic qualities and unusual amber shades which is now a protected species and cannot be used in production. The first natural wood models, with their lovely yellow reflections, were stunning. The 1968 reissues were made of mahogany and painted in a wide range of colours.

Weight was still an issue for solid-body guitars, and this one owes its V-shape to all the parts that were cut out. It is totally aerodynamic, right down to its slightly rounded triangular headstock. The original knobs were made of tulip-shaped plastic. With its cartoon superhero look, it was mad to impress on stage, and over the years it has become a particularly popular choice of guitar for heavy metal players. The design has inspired manufacturers who have made it their speciality, including B.C. Rich, ESP and Jackson.

Gibson Explorer

With its radical, angular shape, the Explorer epitomised the extremes of the rock guitar. It was released in 1957 as an attempt to compete with Fender's Stratocaster. A number of artists, designers and guitar players worked on the prototypes, called Futuras. The audacious shape that was ultimately chosen was officially called the Explorer in 1958. At a price of $247.50, just 40 models were produced, and the first series was withdrawn after a year because of the lack of orders. The Explorer was 20 years ahead of its time, and Hamer Guitars hit the nail on the head when they launched a model paying tribute to the futuristic six-string guitar in 1974. It enjoyed a certain level of success among prog rock musicians, and Gibson made the most of the opportunity to reissue its original model. The Explorer became the guitar of choice for thrash metal guitarists and was copied by manufacturers specialising in the genre such as ESP, Dean Guitars and Jackson.

Gibson Explorer (cherry).

Gibson Explorer (1958).

DEFINITIVE TRACKS

I Will Follow	U2
Sunday Bloody Sunday	U2
One	Metallica
Master of Puppets	Metallica
Free Bird	Lynyrd Skynyrd
Sweet Home Alabama	Lynyrd Skynyrd

Guitar Heroes

For his first good-quality electric guitar, U2's guitarist **The Edge** wanted something a bit different. As a teenager, he happened upon an Explorer in a shop in New York when his eye was caught by the extravagant look. When he returned to Dublin and showed it to Bono, Adam Clayton and Larry Mullen, it was as though he'd brought them something from outer space! The Explorer was a brave choice, as newly formed U2 belonged to the post-punk/new wave movement, and Dave Evans' (otherwise known as The Edge) playing style was a long way away from the hard rock fiends who usually chose this guitar. But his secret trick was to plug it into an echo chamber, opening up the sound to infinity, starting with the band's first album, "Boy", released in 1980. The Edge has stuck with the Explorer for recordings ever since since, and he still uses it on stage along with the dozen or so other models he takes with him on the group's epic tours.

James Hetfield, singer and guitarist with Metallica, is the Explorer's number one fan. Its silhouette sums up the group who invented a thrash version of heavy metal in the 1980s. He carried it very low, with his legs apart, bracing himself over the microphone, as though standing up to the rest of the world. In the early days, he played a Gibson Flying V, before becoming a devotee of the Explorer with its

James Hetfield.

more saturated sound and infinitely more radical look. The best-known of his guitars was white, emblazoned with a sticker saying "More Beer" and fitted with two Seymour Ducan pickups. The second – another white Explorer, but this time made by Japanese company ESP – can be identified by its much more tasteful "Eet Fuk" sticker. Since 1988 and the release of "And Justice for All", James Hetfield and Kirk

Hammett, Metallica's lead guitarist, have had their personal collection with ESP, a fact that doesn't go down too well at Gibson, with the shameless copy of its Explorer.

The band with the greatest density of Explorer fans was the fast and furious trio of **Gary Rossington**, **Allen Collins** and **Steve Gaines**. A fearsome trio with a fiery reputation made up Lynyrd Skynyrd along with singer Ronnie Van Zant. At just 14 years of age, they used to meet at a cabin in the Florida Everglades and played a mixture of country, blues and hard rock which would later be known as Southern Rock. Their hair grew and their personalities hardened. They left school early to set off on the road, touring the seedy bars of the American South. The band's climax was as intense as it was tragic: on 20th October 1977, at the beginning of the tour following the release of the ironically named "Street Survivors" album, Gaines and Van Zant were killed in a plane crash. The survivors kept the legend alive, continuing to play the classic *Sweet Home Alabama* in response to Neil Young who had denounced the state for its racism and slavery, as well as *Free Bird* dedicated to their friend, guitarist Duane Allman. Two rock standards, two hymns to the majesty of their guitars, seamlessly blending together the riffs and the solos of their three Explorers.

TRADE SECRETS

The Explorer was one of the Modernist series made of afara. This rare species contributed to its lightness, and traditional craftsmanship was still respected. When afara became a protected species, it was replaced with mahogany in 1975.
A wider pickguard was introduced to protect the guitar from excessive strumming. Famed for its smooth saturation, the Explorer was never supposed to be played delicately… its two humbuckers guaranteed

satisfying crunch, controlled by two volume knobs but only one tone knob, all lined up as neatly as could be.
With its long, banana-shaped headstock, a first for Gibson, the neck, attached at the 19th fret, offered more than enough access to the high notes. Since 2002 its official name has been x-plorer.

Gibson Firebird

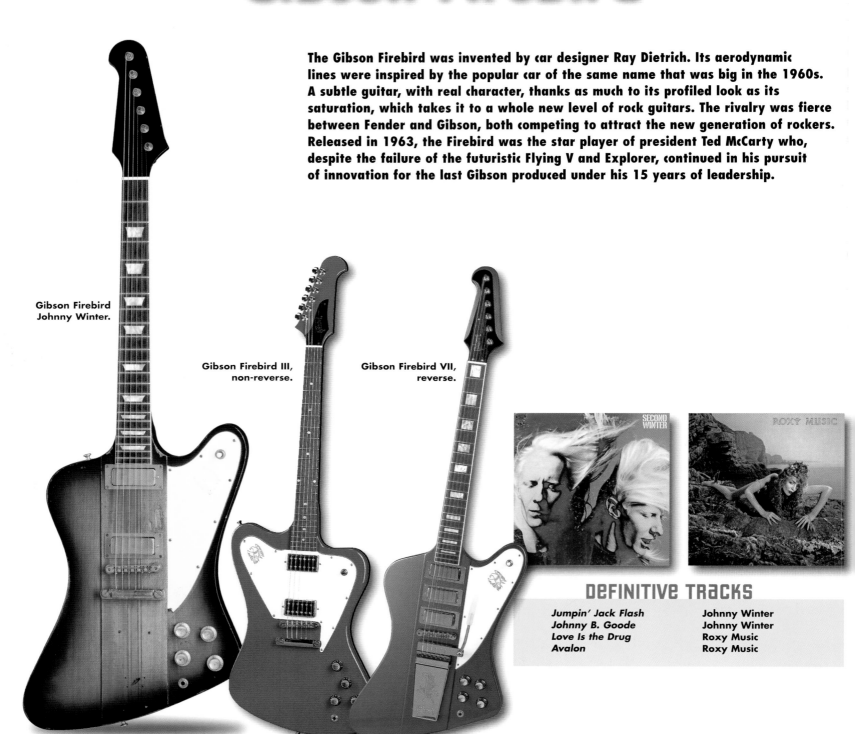

The Gibson Firebird was invented by car designer Ray Dietrich. Its aerodynamic lines were inspired by the popular car of the same name that was big in the 1960s. A subtle guitar, with real character, thanks as much to its profiled look as its saturation, which takes it to a whole new level of rock guitars. The rivalry was fierce between Fender and Gibson, both competing to attract the new generation of rockers. Released in 1963, the Firebird was the star player of president Ted McCarty who, despite the failure of the futuristic Flying V and Explorer, continued in his pursuit of innovation for the last Gibson produced under his 15 years of leadership.

Gibson Firebird Johnny Winter.

Gibson Firebird III, non-reverse.

Gibson Firebird VII, reverse.

DEFINITIVE TRACKS

Jumpin' Jack Flash	Johnny Winter
Johnny B. Goode	Johnny Winter
Love Is the Drug	Roxy Music
Avalon	Roxy Music

Guitar Heroes

Johnny Winter (Johnny Dawson Winter III) was born in Beaumont, Texas, in 1944. He is never without his Firebird, on which he slides unlike any white man of his generation. He learnt to use this famous tube of glass, "the bottleneck", when he was playing with blues musicians in Chicago, the city where he spent his youth with his brother Edgar, another talented musician. Both albinos, they endured their own brand of racism, which stoked their bluesy souls. The whiter than white guitarist became the personification of blues-rock in the 1970s; his name appeared in the line-up for some massive concerts. His repertoire basically covered rock standards with his own personal twist, to the delight of his legions of fans. His Firebird lives up to its name in the album "Captured Live", with his mind-blowing covers of *Jumpin' Jack Flash* and *Johnny B. Goode*. His delicate health, battered by different kinds of abuse (including drugs and alcohol), gradually took him further and further away from the international stage. This guitar hero would return to his musical roots, playing genuine blues music and producing Muddy Waters in the mid 1970s (the most famous version of *Mannish Boy*). Today, Johnny Winter is virtually blind, but he does occasionally appear on stage like a white shadow, letting his legendary Firebird fly once more.

Johnny Winter.

© Fortune-IDOLS/DALLE

The Firebird is a fundamental part of the sound of the most famous British band of the 1970s, Roxy Music, in the hands of guitarist **Phil Manzanera**. With a Columbian mother and an English father, he spent much of his youth in South America, where he learned to play an acoustic guitar. With his dual-culture of pop and Latin American music, he joined Roxy Music in London in 1972. Singer, Bryan Ferry, synthesiser player Brian Eno and drummer Paul Thompson were already in the group, which would enjoy great success with their decadent, experimental rock at the height of the glam rock period. In the 1980s, tired of being Bryan Ferry's glorified backing group, Roxy Music's musicians formed their own group, Explorers. To celebrate 35 years in the business, Manzanera recorded an instrumental album, played exclusively on his favourite guitar. The album, called "Firebird VII", came out in 2008 at the same time as the highly anticipated album hailing Roxy Music's comeback, complete with all the original members, including Brian Eno.

Firebird VII, reverse, 1965 Phil Manzanera.

TRADE SECRETS

The Firebird included a plethora of innovations, including the inverted style of the first series, the reverse body. The revolutionary neck is a single piece, stretching from the headstock right down to the end of the body. This central part is flanked by its winds, giving it a slightly unbalanced weight, with a neck heavier than the body. The headstock, shaped like a bird's beak, is substantial enough to carry the tuners, fitted to the back in a vertical position, like a banjo. The greatest feature of the Firebird is the specially designed mini-humbucker pickups. They are incredibly versatile, producing a clean, clear sound in the high notes and good saturation when the potentiometers are on max.

There's a whole range of Firebirds, including the Firebird I, III, V and VII, plus a 12-string and a bass, called the Thunderbird. Reverse models were made until 1965 before order was restored with a more sensible design, which was not as successful as expected.

Production ended in 1969, before the model was adopted by Johnny Winter, who used it in the 1970s to reinvent his own thrilling version of blues rock.

Jimi Hendrix.

Fender

The Fender brand is recognised around the world, credited for transforming the way music is listened to and produced over the last 50 years. Behind all of the electric guitars, basses and amplifiers, there is one man, a creative genius: Leo Fender was more than just an inventor, he was one of the greatest entrepreneurs of all time, famous for making a massive contribution to the entertainment of millions of people around the globe.

Clarence Leonidas Fender was born in Orange Country, near Los Angeles, on 10th August 1909. He grew up on his parents' ranch, and when he was 13, a student at Fullerton high school, he discovered a passion for electronics: a science that was really starting to take off, which he developed an interest in by tinkering about with radio sets. Armed with his talent and early experience, Leo soon opened a repair shop. At the same time, he used to play the saxophone with a group of musicians including Clayton "Doc" Kauffman, a technician working at Rickenbacker. It wasn't long before the two of them had founded the company K & F and began producing Hawaiian (or lap steel) guitars. When the time came to start borrowing from banks to develop the business, Kauffman jumped ship.

But Leo Fender was an ambitious man. To begin with, he started using a larger building to increase production. In 1947, his friend, George Fullerton joined him. He was a good electrician and a talented guitar player, so he could test the new prototypes. Leo had great faith in his idea of creating an electric guitar without a sound box. The design started out with a very flat piece of wood with a metal plate and a pickup. Fullerton tried the prototype with his band, worked on the sound and made a few adjustments before the pair came up with the final version of the first Fender electric guitar: the Esquire. Small-scale production began on what were first known as Broadcasters, before they were given their definitive name, Telecaster, in 1951.

Soon after that, Fender launched the Precision, the first electric bass. In 1953, new infrastructures and more staff were needed to start a real industrial revolution with the Stratocaster. The efficient production system and quality of the instruments meant that sales quickly took off. More models started to come off the production line, becoming ever more sophisticated, including the Jazzmaster, the Jaguar, the Mustang and the Jazz Bass by 1965. This was the year that Leo Fender's doctor diagnosed him with cancer. He decided to sell his company to CBS for $13 million, then changed doctors… and got better almost immediately! The quality of the instruments produced in the CBS period plummeted, thanks to its intensive production policy.

Released from his non-compete clause in 1974, Leo Fender founded CLF Research and joined forces with Music Man to create the Sabre guitar and the Stingray bass. His last company, G & L (George and Leo), in partnership with his faithful right-hand man George Fullerton, saw a successful return to form with further improvements to the legendary Telecaster and Stratocaster designs.

Leo Fender died on 21st March 1991. He might not have changed the world exactly, but he did make it a better place, for rock lovers at least!

Stratocaster Jeff Beck Surf Green.

Fender Telecaster

In 1946, Leo Fender announced the start of production for electric solid-body guitars and finalised his prototype: a rectangular piece of wood with one pickup and two knobs for volume and tone, which resulted in the Broadcaster in 1950. But Gretsch was already selling a drum kit with the same name, so the marketing campaign was put on hold and for a few months at the beginning of 1951, the new guitars had no name. The transition models are affectionately referred to as Nocasters. Fender came up with the new name, Telecaster, as a nod to the revolutionary guitar's TV appearances. This was a much more appropriate name for the innovative instrument which had remained faithful to its original design.

Success was instant, thanks to its early fans, including the likes of Arthur Smith, Bob Wills and Merle Travis... Could it be that the metallic sound reminded them of the pedal steel and the banjo?

The elegant simplicity of the Telecaster, the mother of all electric guitars, hasn't aged at all. Fans of the Telecaster are an eclectic bunch, covering all genres of music from Muddy Waters' electric blues, via James Burton's country rock, all the way to the out-and-out rock of Keith Richards, Bruce Springsteen, Joe Strummer and Andy Summers – just a few of its most influential players.

In the hands of a talented guitarist, a good Telecaster is worth its weight in gold.

Fender Telecaster
Vintage Hot Rod
1952.

Fender Telecaster
Nocaster Relic
1951.

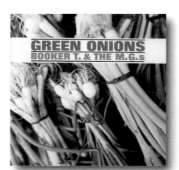

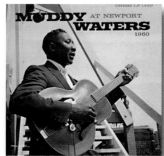

DEFINITIVE TRACKS

The Night Rider	Jimmy Bryant & Speedy West
Elmira Street Boogie	Danny Gatton
Sweet Dreams	Roy Buchanan
You're Still on My Mind	The Byrds
Green Onions	Booker T. & The M.G.s.
Hoochie Coochie Man	Muddy Waters
London Calling	The Clash

Guitar Heroes

Country musicians were fans of the Telecaster from the outset because of its clear, precise notes. **Jimmy Bryant** (1925–1980) was the first guitarist contacted by Fender to try out his invention. With his Western swing style, mingled with a hint of jazz, the "fastest guitar in the country", famous for his pedal steel duets with Speedy West, produced an amazing sound from his "twang machine". Regarded as Midwest America's answer to Django Reinhardt, he was the precursor to the next generation of "Telemasters", as **Danny Gatton** and **Roy Buchanan** were nicknamed. They continued where he had left off, with virtuoso instrumentals which should have earned them greater success than they actually enjoyed, hence their honorary title: "The Best Unknown Guitarists in the World". A special mention should be made of **Albert Lee**, the English guitarist who made a name for himself on the country scene as one of the best guitarists of the genre, playing alongside huge acts including Emmylou Harris and the Everly Brothers.
In the late 1960s, two guitarists with folk-rock band The Byrds, **Clarence White** and **Gram Parsons**, developed the B-Bender which could bend the B string of their Telecasters by a whole tone, making it sound like a pedal steel guitar. This device contributed to The Byrds' return to their country roots, breathing new life into the band which, at the time, was regarded as America's answer to The Beatles.

Clarence White.

Trade Secrets

Traditional acoustic guitars weren't really suited to modern trends, especially at loud volumes, when feedback became a problem. The solution involved reducing the resonance in the sound box with a solid body fitted with electromagnetic pickups, interacting directly with the steel strings.
The only solid-body guitar at that time belonged to Merle Travis, and was designed by Paul Bigsby in 1948. According to George Fullerton, Fender's right-hand man, the specifications were eminently practical: number one, the guitar had to be inexpensive; number two, the neck had to be easy to play and have parts which were easy to change; number three, good pickups. With these criteria, the two men came up with a very flat, light ash body with a cutaway for easy access to the high notes.

The maple neck is made from one piece of wood, attached by four screws, without a separate fingerboard, with the frets pressed directly into the wood. It is strengthened with a metal truss rod which is also used to adjust the tension of the strings. The first models in the series had two pickups: the first on the bridge (single coil) and the second, smaller one, near the neck. There was one volume control and one tone knob, plus a three-way pickup selector switch.
The secret of the characteristic twang sound lies in the bridge pickup, held in place by a piece of metal. The diagonally placed pickup restores the balance between the low notes and the high notes. The closer the pickup is to the neck, the more twang is produced. The second neck pickup has a metal cover, which is supposed to

filter the high notes and give the instrument a more mellow sound.
The advantage that a solid body guitar has over an electric acoustic instrument is its ability to produce a clean sound, without any resonance. The strings cross the sound box and are attached to the back, giving the note a roundness and making it last.
George Fender used to say that Leo Fender insisted that the strings were stretched dead straight, from the bridge to the end of the headstock. It was this faithful colleague who designed the six tuners lined up on the same side of the headstock, inspired by the first guitars made by Martin.

© Dickson-Redferns/DALLE

Muddy Waters.

Steve Cropper, one of the greatest talents of the 1960s and 1970s, highly thought of as a studio musician. With his incisive, funky style, he wasn't the type to get carried away and put notes all over the place – instead, he always managed to find just the right riff to give the song that extra edge. As a producer and arranger for the Stax label in Memphis, he was responsible for classics including *In the Midnight Hour* for Wilson Pickett as well as *(Sittin' on) the Dock of the Bay* for Otis Redding. Next to his burly frame and huge hands, his Telecaster looks tiny in *The Blues Brothers*, which introduced him to the general public in 1980 (soul fans had known about him since 1962 and the famous *Green Onions* by Booker T. & The M.G.s, otherwise known as Stax's house band, with Cropper on guitar!). In the film, he brandished a genuine 1951 Telecaster with a maple neck, one of the sturdiest ever produced by Fender.

In the 1940s, with his heavy, "muddy" style, **Muddy Waters** transformed the rural blues of his elders, Son House and Robert Johnson, into a new energetic style suitable for Chicago's clubs. Using the very early Telecasters, he recorded his classics for the Chess label. He was a massive influence on the 1960s blues generation. Keith Richards and Brian Jones borrowed the title of his signature hit, *Rollin' Stone* for the name of their band. Muddy Waters was also the man behind the traditional rock-group line up (bass, drums, guitar and vocals). The self-titled "father of Chicago blues", passed away in 1983, after a fruitful career spanning 40 years. Members of ZZ Top had a guitar made using some wood taken from the cabin where Muddy Waters had lived as a child: the Muddywood is on display at the Delta Blues Museum in Clarksdale, testimony to the pivotal role that this man had in the history of music.

In 1957, **James Burton**, the worthy heir of Scotty Moore and Carl Perkins, aged just 18, had his first hit, playing lead guitar on Dale Hawkins' *Susie Q.* With his totally unique style, affectionately referred to as "chicken picking", he became a popular guitar player, often invited to play on country rock albums by acts including Buffalo Springfield and Emmylou Harris. But his most prestigious contract was to appear with Elvis Presley in Las Vegas. His Telecaster served him well from 1969 until The King's death in 1977. In 1995, a serious accident left him so badly injured that he couldn't play for a number of years. He has since picked up his red Telecaster once again for a worldwide virtual tour: Elvis The Concert with TCB (Take Care of Business), the original musicians, playing along as images of The King are shown on a big screen.

Joe Strummer (1952–2002) got his Telecaster 66 to emulate the pub rock sound produced by Dr. Feelgood's guitarist Wilko Johnson, who would wave his guitar around like an extra arm, and who was idolised by the future leader of The Clash. He paid $120 for his Telecaster, and took it on stage with his first band, The 101'ers; in April 1976 the Sex Pistols opened for the band at The Nashville Rooms in London. That night, he met the men with whom he would revolutionise rock in the late 1970s: Mick Jones and Paul Simonon. By the end of the concert, Strummer had dumped The 101'ers and joined his new mates. The two guitar players suited each other perfectly: Mick was full of ideas and Joe strummed his Telecaster like nobody's business, hence his surname. The Clash was good to go.
For the next – and tragically final – instalment, take a look at Julien Temple's film *Joe Strummer – The Future Is Unwritten.*

Top: Steve Cropper and James Burton.
Right: Joe Strummer.

Fender Telecaster Esquire

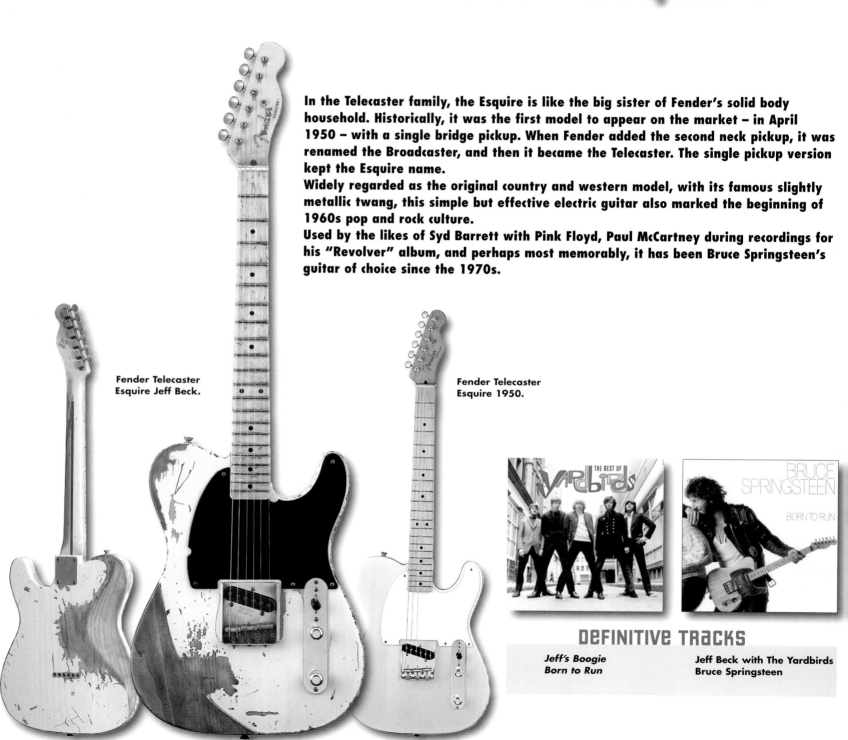

In the Telecaster family, the Esquire is like the big sister of Fender's solid body household. Historically, it was the first model to appear on the market – in April 1950 – with a single bridge pickup. When Fender added the second neck pickup, it was renamed the Broadcaster, and then it became the Telecaster. The single pickup version kept the Esquire name.

Widely regarded as the original country and western model, with its famous slightly metallic twang, this simple but effective electric guitar also marked the beginning of 1960s pop and rock culture.

Used by the likes of Syd Barrett with Pink Floyd, Paul McCartney during recordings for his "Revolver" album, and perhaps most memorably, it has been Bruce Springsteen's guitar of choice since the 1970s.

Fender Telecaster Esquire Jeff Beck.

Fender Telecaster Esquire 1950.

DEFINITIVE TRACKS

Jeff's Boogie
Born to Run

Jeff Beck with The Yardbirds
Bruce Springsteen

© Michael Putland/DALLE

In the full throes of England's 1960s musical boom, **Jeff Beck** bought an Esquire from John "Walker" Maus, guitarist with the Walker Brothers, for $60. With this striking, original 1954 Fender he joined The Yardbirds in 1965 after Eric Clapton's departure. He was quite experimental with his guitar, sometimes using a wah-wah pedal, sometimes playing with the switch to change the tone of his sound, hooked up to a Vox AC30 amp. His use of fuzz on *Heart Full of Soul* was revolutionary. A big fan of Gene Vincent's guitarist, Cliff Gallup, he also demonstrated some rockabilly tendencies on his instrumental *Jeff's Boogie*. Jeff Beck, a friend of Jimi Hendrix, succumbed to the charms of the Stratocaster on *Voodoo Child*. He took his friend's advice and abandoned his Esquire when he left The Yardbirds in 1966 and formed the Jeff Beck Group with Ron Wood and Rod Stewart. The Esquire ended up in the hands of Jimmy Page who had joined Jeff Beck to play with The Yardbirds. The two guitarists can be seen playing seamlessly together in a scene from the film *Blow-Up* by Michelangelo Antonioni.

Bruce Springsteen's Esquire is almost as famous as he is himself, taking pride of place on the cover of "Born to Run", Springsteen's definitive 1975 album.

Rock critic Jon Landau, who would later become his manager, once said: "I've seen rock 'n' roll's future, and its name is Bruce Springsteen". A new American hero, still brandishing his genuine 1954 Esquire, which he bought in 1969 in New Jersey from luthier Phil Petillo for $185.

It's actually a hybrid of two guitars: the body of a Telecaster and the neck of an Esquire. It has had a few modifications over the years: Bruce added a second pickup, and has changed the pickguard a number of times. This unique guitar, which made quite a splash with the E Street Band, is still Springsteen's favourite, although it hasn't been used quite so much since his big comeback in 2003 with the "Rising Tour": The Boss admitted that it kept on going out of tune after a couple of songs, before tuning up again and proving himself worthy of his nickname!

TRADE SECRETS

It was on the Esquire that Leo Fender tried out his famous removable neck, bolted on to the body with four screws. The neck was made from a single piece of wood and so was easy to produce and to remove and replace if it breaks. A revolutionary design for production lines. To avoid waste and make it incredibly easy to play, the neck is extremely thin.

To begin with, the body sculpted out of sturdy ash was a bit thinner than that of the standard Telecaster. But later models would be made in the same was as the Tele, with a two-pickup model and a cavity the size of the sensor. This is what led many guitarists, following in Bruce Springsteen's footsteps, to add a second neck pickup. The Esquire still had a three-way switch — even though it only had a single pickup — to modify the tone, which was used to great effect by the likes of Jeff Beck. Considered to be Fender's bottom-of-the-range model, the Esquire was produced until 1969. After the Fender factories moved to Japan in 1986, it was given a new lease of life with highly popular models.

Fender Telecaster Custom

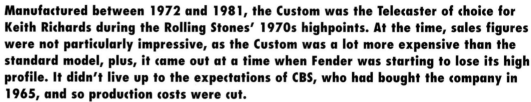

Manufactured between 1972 and 1981, the Custom was the Telecaster of choice for Keith Richards during the Rolling Stones' 1970s highpoints. At the time, sales figures were not particularly impressive, as the Custom was a lot more expensive than the standard model, plus, it came out at a time when Fender was starting to lose its high profile. It didn't live up to the expectations of CBS, who had bought the company in 1965, and so production costs were cut.

The Custom 72, as it is called, to distinguish it from the original Custom produced in the 1950s, was manufactured in Japan, where production quality was reasonably good, and then in Mexico, where it became a slightly cheaper version. According to brand aficionados, the best version would be made in American custom shops, but obviously not for the same price.

Fender Telecaster Custom 72.

DEFINITIVE TRACKS

Roxanne	**Police**
Jumping Jack Flash	**Rolling Stones**
Brown Sugar	**Rolling Stones**

Keith Richards' distinctive early 1970s sound is characterised by two special Telecasters, which contributed to his legendary status. The Micawber 1953 Butterscotch blonde model, and another, with a natural finish, nicknamed Malcolm, from the 1950s. They were both modified and fitted with a neck humbucker, and only had five strings. Keith Richards' signature sound, as heard on *Brown Sugar* and *Jumpin' Jack Flash*, is created by the open G tuning with the low sixth string removed. He learnt the technique from the slide guitar guru, Ry Cooder, in 1968 when he was invited to play on "Beggar's Banquet", the last album which included Brian Jones, who had formed the band in 1962. Classic Stones hits followed, from *Honky Tonk Women* to *Start Me Up*, as exciting to hear as they were to play, earning Keith Richards his nickname as the Human Riff!

Long before he made a name for himself as a rock guitarist with The Police, **Andy Summers** had set off to Los Angeles in 1972 to study classical guitar and get to grips with the subtleties of jazz. He returned to England with a broader mind and a Telecaster Custom which he used for all his different projects, from the progressive jazz rock of Soft Machine, to his psychedelic experiments with Kevin Ayers and Kevin Coyne, right through to the reggae-influenced new wave success of The Police.

He changed the sound of his Telecaster by playing with the treble pickup for syncopated rhythms and using the bass pickup for his forays into jazz.

The rich melodies, usually composed by Sting, were highlighted by Summers' mastery of jazz chords, embellished with echo and harmonies controlled by an impressive effects rack. When he used to talk about his biggest influences, such as Barney Kessel, Wes Montgomery or Django Reinhardt in the early interviews with The Police, Andy Summers bewildered more than one journalist, who at the time thought that this was another punk band.

Over 30 years on, the British band smashed all ticket sales records when they reformed for a world tour in 2007.

To play like one of the Rolling Stones, you don't need much: a good vintage Telecaster plugged into an all-tube Twin Reverb amplifier… plus of course it helps if you're a riff expert like **Keith Richards**, with a long apprenticeship spanning 40 years, spent endlessly studying Robert Johnson's blues and Chuck Berry's rock 'n' roll.

TRADE SECRETS

The Fender Telecaster Custom produced in 1972 came with a more extensive range of sounds than the traditional Telecaster.

It had two pickups with different characteristics. A single coil for the bridge pickup, and a wide-range humbucker for the neck. So the much more flexible Telecaster Custom combined the traditional crystal-clear sound with the denser sound that was popular in the 1970s.

The Custom model used by The Police's guitarist Andy Summers is the perfect example of this, with his clean jazz asides along with the rockier bits with their heavy saturation. Using wide range pickups, made by Seth Lover, the creator of the two-coil pickup, Fender attempted to win back customers who had been seduced by the more powerful Gibson sound.

Fender Telecaster Deluxe

Since it was created in 1950, the Telecaster hasn't changed much, but it has nevertheless had to adapt to new musical trends. In the 1970s, with the growing popularity of rock, a bigger sound, becoming heavier and heavier, was popular with guitarists. In 1972, Fender responded to this with the Deluxe, regarded as the top-of-the-range Telecaster and in direct competition with the heavy sound of Gibsons. Produced until 1982, this particular Telecaster model has enjoyed a revival in the new millennium. It has become one of the coolest and most popular guitars ever since the new indie rock generation adopted it.

Radiohead's Thom York, Franz Ferdinand's Alex Kapranos and Blur's Graham Coxon all play with the Telecaster Deluxe.

Fender Telecaster Deluxe 72 black.

Fender Telecaster Deluxe 72 walnut.

DEFINITIVE TRACKS

Take Me Out	Franz Ferdinand
Creep	Radiohead

Guitar Heroes

Radiohead, the most popular rock band on the planet between 1990 and 2000, is also one of the most experimental, which is handy for the creativity of a group with such a concentration of guitars.

They were particularly fond of Fender guitars, including the 1973 Telecaster Deluxe, covered in stickers, which belonged to the group's figurehead, **Thom Yorke**.

Since it was formed in 1987, Radiohead's output has been constantly evolving, taking inspiration from electronic music, jazz and even classical music, without ever losing its exciting, modern edge, attracting new fans and retaining hardcore ones.

Thom Yorke's band has enjoyed success ever since its first album, thanks to the single *Creep*; guitarist Jonny Greenwood says that he deliberately messed up the chords in the chorus because he thought the song was depressing. And it was precisely this air of frustration, alternating between crystal clear arpeggios and outbursts of saturated sound, that proved popular.

Radiohead have always steered clear of the easy way to success by remaining incredibly demanding when it comes to the band's musical direction. The music business is closely controlled, but Radiohead has frequently adopted unconventional strategies, going so far as to release their last album,

"In Rainbows" online, for whatever price fans wanted to pay for it.

Rock was back on the dancefloor at the dawn of the millennium, with Scottish band Franz Ferdinand, competing on a level playing field with the powerful beat of electronic music without compromising the traditional formula of a rock band favoured by The Kinks and The Who. Armed with his 1972 Telecaster Deluxe, charismatic guitarist and singer **Alex Kapranos**, has the same dark, strident sound as Gang of Four and Wire, two bands which led the new wave in the post-punk and disco in the early 1980s. Somewhat removed from the Britpop phenomenon and electronic trends, Franz Ferdinand cultivated their dandyish image in their hangout in Glasgow, ironically nicknamed The Château. A venue for partying and for work, decorated in the style of Andy Warhol's Factory.

© Roger Wong /INFGoff/DALLE

Franz Ferdinand.

TRADE SECRETS

The crystal-clear sound and lack of sustain boasted by the Telecaster went out of favour in the 1970s. The solution was to fit the Deluxe with a couple of two-coil pickups with a thicker sound.

Fender approached Seth Lover, the man who had invented the highly popular humbucker for Gibson, to adapt its guitars. The result was the wide range pickup used on many Fenders, including the Custom, the Thinline and even the semi-acoustic model, the Starcaster.

Produced between 1972 and 1981, this particular Telecaster is immediately recognisable because it's the only one with a headstock like the Stratocaster. That's not the only thing it has in common with the Strat: the neck is the same too, with its 21 frets, and the body has similar rounded contours. The four volume and tone controls are similar too. Some Deluxes are also fitted with the famous Strat tremolo arm. In 2004, Fender reissued the Deluxe model, identical to the 1970s model in every way.

Fender Stratocaster

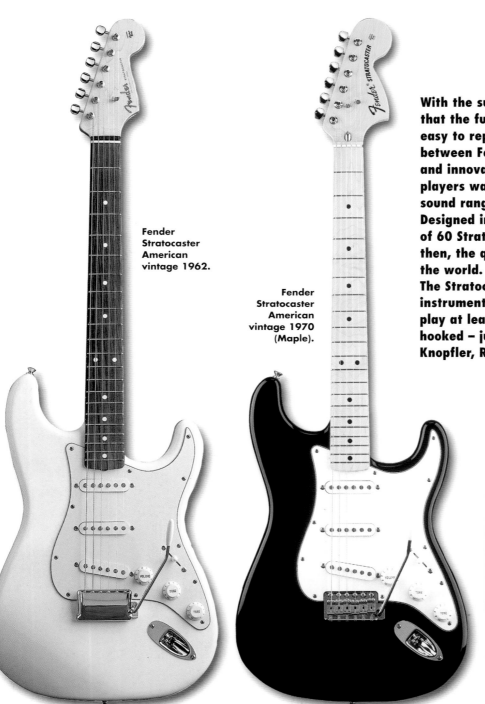

Fender
Stratocaster
American
vintage 1962.

Fender
Stratocaster
American
vintage 1970
(Maple).

With the success of the Telecaster, Leo Fender was convinced that the future lay in the solid-body guitar; mass-produced and easy to repair. The Stratocaster was the result of a collaboration between Fender and musicians who really cared about comfort and innovation. Playing methods were evolving and guitar players wanted to be more at ease on stage with a greater sound range with the same guitar.

Designed in 1953 by Leo Fender and George Fullerton, a batch of 60 Stratocasters were first produced in spring 1954. Since then, the queen of electric guitars has sold in its millions around the world.

The Stratocaster is undeniably one of the mythical six-string instruments that any self-respecting guitar player really has to play at least once in his or her life. Play it once and you'll be hooked – just ask Jimi Hendrix, Eric Clapton, Jeff Beck, Mark Knopfler, Rory Gallagher, Stevie Ray Vaughan...

DEFINITIVE TRACKS

All Along the Watchtower	Jimi Hendrix
Shine on You Crazy Diamond	Pink Floyd

Guitar Heroes

Pink Floyd guitarist, **David Gilmour** owned the very first commercially available "Strat", no. 0001, which came off the production line in 1954. David Gilmour's technician bought it for $900 from Leo Fender himself.

In 1968, David Gilmour replaced his friend Syd Barrett who was suffering from mental problems caused by too much acid. His skills as a guitarist were described as "stratospheric" following his stunning solo in *Echoes*, which took up the whole B-side of the group's "Meddle" album (1971). This ethereal track marked a turning point in Pink Floyd's career thanks to Gilmour's bluesy playing on his famous 1969 Black Strat. He got his hands on this other legendary guitar in New York, from Manny's, a famous music store with illustrious customers including Jimi Hendrix. In 1973, this Strat was fitted with a humbucker pickup for the recording of "The Dark Side of the Moon", widely considered to be the epitome of 1970s prog rock.

In 1977, Gilmour had the more saturated DiMarzio pickups fitted for the album "The Wall" and the epic tour that followed. Time and again, the same Stratocaster was given a brand new sound, always played with great sensitivity.

Hardcore guitar geeks might also be interested to know that the famous solo

on *Another Brick in the Wall* wasn't in fact played on the beloved Stratocaster, but rather on a 1955 Gibson Les Paul Gold Top with an old P-90!

Jimi Hendrix and the Stratocaster were a match made in heaven. Although he played on other guitars, he was the undisputed master of the Strat. The Voodoo Child was ambidextrous: he wrote with his right hand but played with his left. But he insisted on right-handed Stratocasters, played upside down with the nut the wrong way round so that the E string was on the bottom and the knobs were on top. Hendrix had several dozen that he adapted himself. He didn't actually make too many adjustments to his instruments as they had a limited lifespan. Some were hand-painted, like the one that he burned on stage at the Monterey Festival in June 1967. Contrary to popular belief, Hendrix only set light to two or three throughout his career, one of which was acquired and kept by Frank Zappa. Most were exclusive models made from putting together parts of the different Strats that he had ruined on stage. Of the 100 or so guitars that the icon ever owned, there is one that is perhaps even more valuable than all the others: the very last one, nicknamed Black Beauty, used in September 1970 just before his death. It was kept for a long time by his last girlfriend, Monika: nobody has dared lay a finger on its sacred strings since the day it left Hendrix's hands…

David Gilmour, 1984.

TRADE SECRETS

At the request of guitar players themselves, the Stratocaster was the first solid-body guitar with three pickups. It was also the first to benefit from the double cutaway design which made the high notes in the upper frets easier to get to.

Leo Fender was a true master of his craft, creating pickups that could be used separately or together. As he wasn't a guitarist himself, it was Bill Carson who tested them. He also helped to design the contours of the body and the shape of the back to make it more comfortable, along with another country artist, Rex Galleon. Fender's third consultant was Freddie Tavares, the great steel guitar player, who concentrated on the integrity of the vibrato.

The first users were once again country musicians as well as jazz artists like Alvino Rey and great blues players such as Johnny "Guitar" Watson. But it was the advent of rock 'n' roll and the impact of the likes of Buddy Holly and Gene Vincent in 1956 that really made the Strat take off.

Fender Stratocaster Fiesta Red

Fender Stratocaster Fiesta Red signature Mark Knopfler.

Mark Knopfler Stratocaster®

Comfort Contoured, '57 Lightweight Ash Body
Vintage, Tinted '62 "C" Shape Maple Neck
Fender®/Gotoh® Vintage-Style Tuning Machines
3 Texas Special™, Single-Coil Strat Pickups
American Vintage Synchronized Tremolo
5-Way Switching • 21 Medium Jumbo Frets
Rosewood Fingerboard

Fender
THE SPIRIT OF ROCK-N-ROLL™

The legendary Stratocaster came out in 1954 and has not fundamentally changed since then. The prototype was referred to as the Bill Carson model, named after the famous country guitarist who used to test guitars for the company, but its aerodynamic shape soon earned it the title of the Stratocaster, referring to the B-52 Stratofortress, a symbol of the modern approach to design that was becoming popular in the 1950s. The shape of the Strat is similar to that of the Precision, the first electric bass released by Fender a few years earlier. Players' comfort was a priority, with a cutaway in the back that sits more comfortably on the hip and is easier on the forearm. Shamelessly copied by other manufacturers, the Stratocaster is the ultimate template for the electric guitar.

DEFINITIVE TRACKS

That'll Be the Day	Buddy Holly
Apache	The Shadows
Sultans of Swing	Dire Straits

Mark Knopfler.

The rise in popularity of the Stratocaster, which until then had only been fully appreciated by the country and blues scene, was boosted by **Buddy Holly**'s TV appearances. In the space of two years between 1957 and 1958, the bespectacled young rocker and his Crickets produced a series of hits including *That'll Be the Day*, which owe a great deal to the strident sound of the Stratocaster. Buddy had three or four of them during his short career. The last one wasn't actually red, it was a '58 Sunburst which is now on show at the museum dedicated to him in his birth town, Lubbock in Texas. He was playing this guitar at the concert he gave just before the airplane crash that cost him his life on 3rd February 1959. He was just 22 years old.

Hank Marvin, guitarist with The Shadows, was the first European musician to play on a Stratocaster imported from the United States in 1959. Cliff Richard, the brand new idol of young English girls, accompanied by The Shadows, ordered him Buddy Holly's guitar, the most expensive in the Fender catalogue ($120 at the time). Playing with the tremolo arm from his Fiesta Red Strat, Hank accidentally discovered the sound which became The Shadows' trademark with the instrumental track *Apache*, which went on to become number one around the world in 1960, the first of a long series of hits which inspired countless artists, from Frank Zappa to Neil Young, not to mention Mark Knopfler. Another feature of the Hank Marvin sound is the use of the famous Vox AC30 amplifier, which was made in England, and which he helped to develop. An amp that was later made even more popular when it was used by The Beatles and The Rolling Stones.

Mark Knopfler's virtuosity worked perfectly with the clear sound of the Stratocaster, contrasting with the heavy sound which was so popular in the 1970s. As a child, Dire Straits' guitarist dreamed of a red guitar that he'd seen in the window of a music shop: the model used by Hank Marvin. This Fiesta Red became the symbol of his old-fashioned, refined playing style, following in the footsteps of J. J. Cale and Chet Atkins. Mark Knopfler was working as a journalist when, aged 27, he decided to pursue his musical dream. A demo was sent to the BBC, who played the track *Sultans of Swing* every night. As a result, the band was signed by Vertigo and went on to become one of the biggest-selling groups of the 1980s.
As for the Fiesta Red from his childhood: it became Fender's Mark Knopfler signature model.

TRADE SECRETS

The first Stratocasters were blonde or sunburst. In 1956, so-called custom finishes started to appear, in a whole array of bright colours. George Fullerton discovered the red colour in a paint shop by mixing several shades, and he used this mix on the prototype of the Jazzmaster. His colleagues thought it was a crazy idea, but he persisted and used it on the Stratocaster too.
Leo Fender offered the red model to Pee Wee Crayton, the first blues musician to play on a Strat for his two big classics *You Know Yeah* and *The Telephone Is Ringing*.
The model really took off when English guitarist Hank Marvin, virtuoso guitarist with The Shadows, Cliff Richards' backing group, adopted the Fiesta Red.

Fender Stratocaster Signatures

Fender became experts in producing signature models, or Relics, in their Custom workshops. You can now pretend you're rubbing shoulders with a legend, with Rory Gallagher's tortoiseshell Strat, Clapton's Blackie, Stevie Ray Vaughan's Number One, Buddy Guy's blues guitar or Yngwie Malmsteen's scalloped fingerboard.

As well as the care taken over the look and finish, French musician Paul Personne confirms that these copies sound brilliant too – so there's no need to worry about tracking down a collector's model when there are these versions around which are just as good as the originals!

Fender Strastocaster signature Eric Clapton (Blackie Relic).

Fender Strastocaster signature Stevie Ray Vaughan.

Fender Strastocaster signature Rory Gallagher.

RORY GALLAGHER the bullfrog interlude

ERIC CLAPTON SLOWHAND

STEVIE RAY VAUGHAN

The Sky Is Crying

DEFINITIVE TRACKS

Cocaine	Eric Clapton
Bullfrog Blues	Rory Gallagher
The Sky Is Crying	Stevie Ray Vaughan

Guitar Heroes

In early 1970, one of England's most idolised guitarists, **Eric Clapton**, was 25 years old when he released his first eponymous solo album. With the crystal-clear sound of his 1957 sunburst Stratocaster, his style was calmer and more laid back. It was with this very guitar, nicknamed Brownie, that he produced the masterpiece *Layla*, under the pseudonym Derek & The Dominos, which includes some memorable sparring with fellow guitarist Duane Allman.

While on tour, Clapton popped into the Sho-Bud store in Nashville. He stocked up with six 1956 vintage Stratocasters and gave three of them to his friends George Harrison, Steve Winwood and Pete Townshend. He kept the other three, picked the best bits from each one and created a unique Stratocaster, nicknamed Blackie, his guitar of choice for the next 15 years or so.

One night, after a fair amount of Jamaican rum, as he was recording the album "461 Ocean Boulevard", Eric collapsed, drunk, on his Strat and broke it in two. It was repaired without too much damage, but it was too fragile to take on tour. Fender started making limited edition copies in 1987. The original Blackie was put up for auction at Christie's in 2004 to raise money for the Crossroads rehab centre founded by Eric Clapton: it was sold for nearly a million dollars.

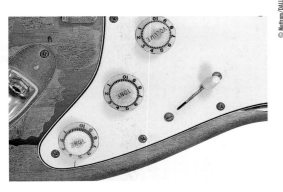

TRADE SECRETS

The profile of the Stratocaster is immediately synonymous with the electric guitar, but when you look a bit more closely, you'll see that there are dozens of different versions. There have been so many series over the years that it would take forever to list them here. There are an infinite number of combinations, mixtures of standards and one-off designs.

The **Stevie Ray Vaughan** phenomenon breathed new life into traditional blues, counteracting the new wave synth movement of the 1980s. His best friend was a 1959 Stratocaster whose finish had been worn away by the sweaty atmosphere of the blues clubs in Austin, Texas, his adopted home. His Number One was fitted with three Texas Special pickups and a pickguard engraved with his initials. The Texan had a left-handed tremolo arm fitted at the top of the bridge so that it was more accessible, and he tuned it half a tone down, just like Jimi Hendrix, who had a huge influence on him.

In 1982, Stevie Ray made a big splash at the Montreux festival before he'd been signed to any particular label. David Bowie was in the audience, and hired him there and then for "Let's Dance", while Jackson Browne offered his studios free of charge for the recording of his first album. It was the beginning of an amazing decade for Stevie Ray, and he was soon hailed by six-string kings such as Eric Clapton, Jeff Beck, Buddy Guy and B. B. King who saw in him their spiritual heir. Tragically, on 27th August 1990, after a final concert with a host of artists (including Clapton, Guy and Robert Cray), his helicopter crashed in thick fog and he was killed instantly.

His posthumous album was poignantly entitled, "The Sky Is Crying".

Humble and unpretentious, **Rory Gallagher** was a genuine rockstar from Ireland. Brought up on folk and rock 'n' roll, he won a talent competition in his native Cork when he was just 15 years old. He could finally afford his stunning 1961 sunburst Stratocaster which he had been dreaming about for ages. It cost £100, a small fortune at the time, but this guitar would accompany him throughout his career. It was allegedly the first Strat to be sold in Ireland. A keen fan of blues rock, he was an artist who was most at home on stage. The British press named him musician of the year when his "Live in Europe" album was released in 1972.

Over the years, after thousands of concerts, his Stratocaster began to show signs of wear and tear; its neck was badly twisted, and it turned out that Gallagher's perspiration was a bit too acidic for the varnish! His whole personality was tied up with his guitar which was impregnated with his blood, sweat and tears. Gallagher died after years of drugs and alcohol abuse, despite a liver transplant, when he was just 47 on 14th June 1994.

Designed by master luthier John English, Fender marketed a signature model which was the exact replica of his original Strat, down to the last scratch.

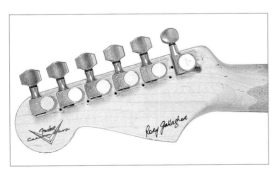

Fender Jazzmaster

Fender
Jazzmaster
Jay Mascis
Dinosaur Jr.

Designed in 1958 as a top-of-the-range model for the Fender catalogue, as the name suggests, the Jazzmaster was initially aimed at professional jazz musicians. Its asymmetric ergonomics were specially designed so that it could be played sitting down, with a clear, warm, rounded sound.

Paradoxically, the modern lines and rich sounds were a hit with guitarists playing surf music – the latest craze in the early 1960s on the America's West Coast: the Jazzmaster was at the forefront of this musical trend, which was dominated by the tremolo effects favoured by The Ventures, who had a number 1 in 1961 with *Walk Don't Run*. It went out of fashion in the 1970s, but when it was withdrawn from the catalogue in 1977, a new generation of artists discovered this prestigious guitar, which was fairly affordable by now. Elvis Costello, Tom Verlaine (Television) and Robert Smith (The Cure) were all won over by the strident sound of the Jazzmaster and its retro/futuristic look. They would later be copied by New York band Sonic Youth, who made it the symbolic guitar of avant-garde rock.

DEFINITIVE TRACKS

Walk Don't Run	The Ventures
Marquee Moon	Television
Dirty Boots	Sonic Youth

Guitar Heroes

Like many young musicians of his era – the second half of the 1970s – **Tom Verlaine** confesses that he bought this guitar because of the low price. He was quickly won over by the strident sound of the Jazzmaster because it reminded him of the distorted notes that his hero, John Coltrane, managed to produce with his saxophone. A fan of poetry, the young Thomas Miller borrowed his stage name from Paul Verlaine when he arrived in New York with his friend Richard Hell. Together, they laid the foundations for a new genre of poetic, urbane music with Television, formed in 1975. They were regulars at famous underground club, CBGB, where punk and new wave were born with The Ramones, Blondie and Talking Heads.

The first album, "Marquee Moon", was hailed as a work of genius by critics who were captivated by Tom Verlaine's plaintive vocals and the revolutionary guitar parts plated on his Jazzmaster. The unusual chords, inspired by jazz with a hint of psychedelia, influenced countless young guitar players including U2's The Edge and The Cure's Robert Smith.

In 2000, on a famous auction website, Tom Verlaine's Jazzmaster was sold for $31,000 – a bit more than the $150 for which he bought it in 1974!

New York band **Sonic Youth** have got through their fair share of Jazzmasters in their time. They have owned dozens of them, with different tunings specific to each track and often modified to create brand new sounds. Formed in 1981 as part of the no wave scene, by guitarists Thurston Moore and Lee Ranaldo and bass player Kim Gordon, the band was influenced by the experimental music of composer Glenn Branca with whom they started out. Although incredibly knowledgeable about rock culture, they painstakingly deconstructed their pop compositions with distortion and dissonance to achieve a certain form of free jazz at a very loud volume. Sonic Youth has

© Aquilino/DALLE

Thurston Moore.

had a huge influence on the indie rock scene, leading the way for countless bands, the most famous of which would have to be Nirvana.

TRADE SECRETS

When the Jazzmaster was created in 1958, Fender had no idea that it was providing an instrument for hardcore rockers. The idea was rather to create a sophisticated guitar with a light, alder body. It was the first Fender with a rosewood fingerboard instead of a one-piece maple neck. The electronics were particularly complex with an elaborate set of controls so that the tone could be changed quickly.

For surf music, the most important thing was the floating tremolo and its tremolo lock to keep the guitar from going out of tune in any situation.

This guitar is full of character which made it popular with alternative rock groups. It owes its distinctive sound to its two single-coil jazz pickups inspired by Gibson's P-90s. The warmth and depth of the sound are offset by a bit of feedback. Some musicians complain about this, while

others are more than happy to work around it, like Jay Mascis from Dinosaur Jr., Thurston Moore and Lee Ranaldo from Sonic Youth and Kevin Shields from My Bloody Valentine, who turned it into a feature, creating what rock critics dubbed "noise pop" in the early 1990s.

Fender Jaguar

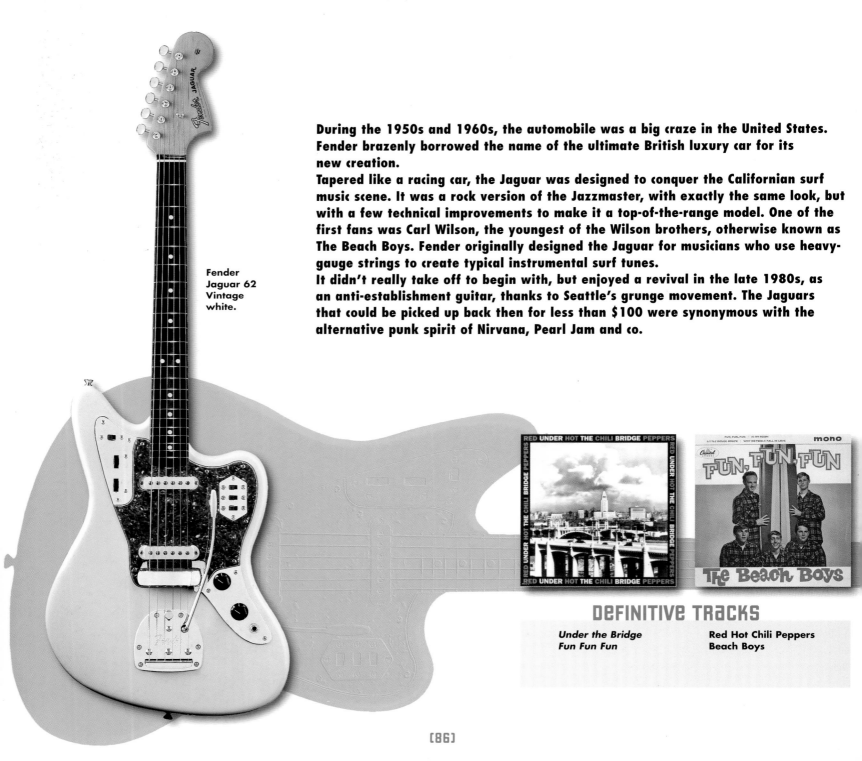

Fender
Jaguar 62
Vintage
white.

During the 1950s and 1960s, the automobile was a big craze in the United States. Fender brazenly borrowed the name of the ultimate British luxury car for its new creation.

Tapered like a racing car, the Jaguar was designed to conquer the Californian surf music scene. It was a rock version of the Jazzmaster, with exactly the same look, but with a few technical improvements to make it a top-of-the-range model. One of the first fans was Carl Wilson, the youngest of the Wilson brothers, otherwise known as The Beach Boys. Fender originally designed the Jaguar for musicians who use heavy-gauge strings to create typical instrumental surf tunes.

It didn't really take off to begin with, but enjoyed a revival in the late 1980s, as an anti-establishment guitar, thanks to Seattle's grunge movement. The Jaguars that could be picked up back then for less than $100 were synonymous with the alternative punk spirit of Nirvana, Pearl Jam and co.

DEFINITIVE TRACKS

Under the Bridge	Red Hot Chili Peppers
Fun Fun Fun	Beach Boys

Guitar Heroes

Surf music was at the top of the charts between 1960 and 1963, with largely instrumental groups like Dick Dale & The Deltones, The Surfaris and The Ventures. Then came The Beach Boys, with their irresistible pop songs and their sumptuous vocal harmonies. For half a dozen years, **Carl Wilson**, his brothers (Dennis and Brian) and their cousin Mike Love produced a series of huge hits from *Surfin' USA* in 1962 to the 1967 hymn to flower power, *Good Vibrations*. In Carl Wilson's hands, the Jaguar accompanied the first years of The Beach Boys' pure surf years. Things were cranked up a notch or two with *I Get Around* which revealed Brian Wilson's musical genius. The Beach Boys were soon overwhelmed by the huge English wave that was sweeping the world, led by The Beatles. A musical harmony war began, with Brian Wilson and his "Pet Sounds" (1966) and Paul McCartney who responded with "Sgt. Pepper's Lonely Hearts Club Band" (1967), two albums which fought it out for a place at the top of the perfect pop parade. The Beach Boys' lead guitarist, Carl Wilson, also provided the vocals for *God Only Knows*, one of their finest songs, and he also started producing for the group in the late 1960s, although he would never quite catch up with his brother's success. He died in February 1998.

In 1988, **John Frusciante** was just 17 when he joined the Red Hot Chili Peppers, replacing

John Frusciante.

their first guitarist, Hillel Slovak, who had died from an overdose. He had recently auditioned for Frank Zappa but, slightly baffled by the latter's seriousness, he hadn't been able to bring himself to play a single note. With the Red Hot Chili Peppers, he discovered a rather off-the-wall spirit with which he felt much more comfortable. Frusciante found some of the funk metal parts demanded of him a bit tricky when they were recording "Mother's Milk". The album was good and it was very successful, but it didn't really capture the band's spirit. Their minds were already on the ambitious "Blood Sugar Sex Magic" with producer Rick Rubin.

John's clear, ethereal playing on his 1962 Ocean turquoise Jaguar can be heard on *Under the Bridge*, the track which catapulted the band into superstardom. Frusciante felt uncomfortable with this phenomenal success and wasn't getting on brilliantly with the rest of the band, so he withdrew and backed out of the Japanese tour in 1992. He spent the next six years painting and recording solo albums, living a rather isolated life. Bass player Flea and singer Anthony Kiedis rescued him from the edge of the abyss and recreated the winning formula of the Red Hot Chili Peppers. The resulting album, "Californication", put the band back on the right track in 1999. Frusciante was back to form, now with another 1962 Jaguar – a Fiesta Red!

TRADE SECRETS

Introduced in 1962, the Jaguar was the first Fender with 22 frets on the neck instead of the usual 24. The maple neck had a rosewood fingerboard like the Jazzmaster, with the same asymmetric shape carved out of alder. The two single-coil pickups are very similar to the Strat's, but protected with a strip of notched metal plates. The controls are a complex dual-circuit system, lead and rhythm, controlled by a number of switches, including one positioned on a diamond-shaped plate producing a high-pitched tone, which is particularly suited to surf music. There was also a patented spring-loaded rubber Fender Mute for the strings. These significant improvements justified the extortionate price of $379.50 for the Jaguar, a guitar destined to become the ultimate instrument for the golden age of surf music.

Fender Mustang

Fender Mustang 65 (Daphne Blue).

The Mustang was launched in 1964 onto a booming market, as a student model. Its short 22-fret neck is adapted to be held by young musicians just starting out on their musical careers.

In its category, it was head and shoulders above other guitars with more features, and was excellent value for money at the time, costing just $159.50.

With its irresistible pastel Daphne Blue, Dakota Red or Surf Green finishes, and its pearly pickguard, it's still popular with collectors who are prepared to pay up to $1,500 for one. The Mustang experienced a revival in the 1980s. The American alternative music scene fell in love with this vintage model and fans included David Byrne (Talking Heads), Frank Black (Pixies), Thurston Moore and Lee Ranaldo (Sonic Youth), and of course, Kurt Cobain, who got through his fair share by smashing them up on stage at the end of Nirvana's energetic gigs...

Fender Mustang Competition.

DEFINITIVE TRACKS

Love Buzz	Nirvana
Smells Like Teen Spirit	Nirvana
Lithium	Nirvana
Heart Shaped Box	Nirvana

Guitar Heroes

For his 14th birthday, **Kurt Cobain** could choose between a bicycle or a guitar and amp. He didn't think twice, and was soon taking lessons and learning to play AC/DC songs. Kurt was left-handed, and because suitable models were rare, he started playing right-handed guitars with the strings fitted the opposite way around.

His favourite guitar was a 1969 Competition Mustang with a Lake Placid Blue finish, which he bought soon before he recorded "Nevermind", the band's triumphant 1991 album. It was this guitar that he was playing during the video for *Smells Like Teen Spirit* that captivated Generation X. He acquired the habit of smashing it up at the end of Nirvana's concerts, amidst the screams and hysteria of the audience. All of his Mustangs, Fiesta Reds and Sonic Blues, were picked up second-hand for next to nothing; he bought his first Mustang for $20, and used it to record the first album, "Bleach", which was made for less than $600. Quite a leap to the million-dollar icon that he has become today, but it fitted in with the punk ethos that he championed right to the

end. His painful battle for honesty ended with his death on 5th April 1994.

In his diaries, filled with scrawling ramblings, little sketches and lists of his favourite rock songs, Kurt drew his perfect guitar. A hybrid model which he labelled the Jag-Stand

Fender Jag-Stand (Sonic Blue).

which boasted the best of his two favourite guitars, the Jaguar for the top part and the Mustang for the bottom. Fender produced a prototype for him which he used on his last tour, but he wasn't 100% satisfied with it. The Jag-Stand, with its slightly unbalanced curves, was released after his death.

TRADE SECRETS

Make no mistake, the Mustang has the genuine Fender sound, with two angled single-coil pickups, which is why it is so sought-after. It bears comparison with the label's big names with its clear sound when plugged into a Marshal amp producing satisfying saturation. Fender's cheaper models began in 1956 with the Musicmaster, fitted with a single pickup and no tremolo arm, and the Duo-Sonic with two pickups. The Mustang

was actually a follow-on from these two guitars with the same design. The main novelty was the Dynamic Vibrato with six-bridge saddles, known for its quality, with a smoother action.

For those really in the know, the Mustang Competition series are the ones to look out for. Produced from 1968 until 1973, available in red, blue or orange with the headstock painted the same colour, they are easily

identified by the white strips painted on the body. A must for those nostalgic for the 1960s.

The last model produced under Leo Fender's rule was the Mustang Bass. In 1965, he sold the business to CBS for health reasons. The company on the other hand was incredibly healthy, revitalised by sales for its guitars which were by now so popular with rockers.

Fender Precision Bass

Fender
American
Standard
Precision Bass.

Always keen to hear musicians' opinions, Leo Fender invented the first electric bass, the Precision, designed as a counterpart to the Telecaster. It meant that bass players could be heard as well as being able to move around more freely with their instruments.

The electric bass is a relatively recent creation. Before it came along, double basses, played upright, provided the bass line. Despite their size, they couldn't always be heard in orchestras. In the 1930s, Rickenbacker had an amplified bass, and then there was the Audiovox, the first small electric bass by Paul Tutmarc. But the first actual electric guitar to be mass-produced was the Precision in 1951. It was called the Precision because it had 20 frets so that notes could be played more precisely, unlike the fretless double bass. The electric P-Bass came at the perfect moment to produce a solid rhythm, and its advent contributed to the emergence of rock 'n' roll. It soon became the most popular bass in all genres of amplified music.

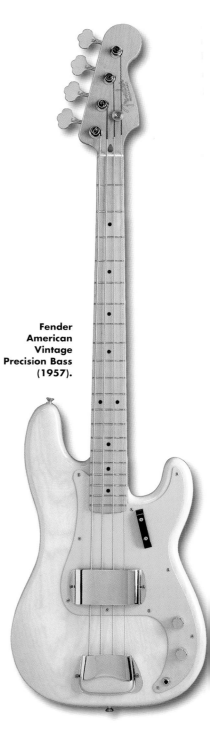

Fender
American
Vintage
Precision Bass
(1957).

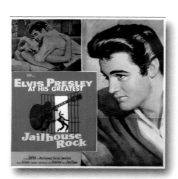

DEFINITIVE TRACKS

Jailhouse Rock	Elvis Presley
What's Going On	Marvin Gaye
Roxanne	Police

Bass Heroes

Fender's order book was soon overflowing after Elvis's bassist, **Bill Black**, recorded *Jailhouse Rock* in 1957 with a Precision. Regarded as the first rock hit using an electric bass, its appearance in the film of the same name gave its popularity a massive boost. Producers were still finding it difficult to cope without a double bass in the studio, so the electric bass was used as a backing instrument on Duane Eddy's instrumental *Rebel Rouser* in 1958.

Carole Kaye, the "First Lady of Bass", started out as a guitarist but when a bassist didn't turn up for a recording in 1963, she stepped in. The rest was history – with her Precision, she soon became one of the most sought-after session musicians in Los Angeles. Her distinctive style, using a plectrum for the first time, can be heard on a number of hits by Quincy Jones, Phil Spector, Ray Charles and The Beach Boys.

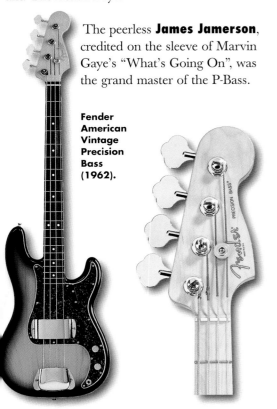

The peerless **James Jamerson**, credited on the sleeve of Marvin Gaye's "What's Going On", was the grand master of the P-Bass.

Fender American Vintage Precision Bass (1962).

Starting out on the jazz scene, he picked up an electric bass when he joined the Funk Brothers for the Motown label. Armed with his funk machine, he played on hundreds of tracks between 1962 and 1968, including 30 or so number ones by Stevie Wonder, The Four Tops, The Temptations and The Supremes.

Gordon Sumner, the son of a milkman from Newcastle, started to get into music with a guitar he had inherited from his uncle. When he started playing bass, he began to make a name for himself in his hometown in a jazz orchestra; on stage, he can often be seen wearing a bright yellow striped jumper, making him look like a giant bumble bee. It was during this period that he acquired his nickname: **Sting**. In London in 1976, he and drummer Stewart Copeland founded The Police, in the height of the punk movement, along with Andy Summers on the guitar. The band enjoyed massive success, selling more than 50 million albums. After an unofficial break-up, the trio embarked on a triumphant tour in 2007. For the record-breaking run of concerts, Sting played an old sunburst Precision bass, which he never even paid for:

it's the one that was used in the video for *Demolition Man*, a Police song that he re-recorded for the soundtrack of the film of the same name starring Sylvester Stallone in 1993. To match the desolate décor of the video set, a member of the crew was sent out into town to pick up the most battered old bass he could find. The one he found was one of the very first Precisions from 1954, whose body was modelled on the Telecaster and which had a single-coil pickup. A highly collectable guitar that had only just escaped the scrapheap became Fender's signature Sting model!

TRADE SECRETS

Back in 1951, the original shape was inspired by the Telecaster with an ash body and a blonde finish. After a number of tests, the Precision's neck, halfway between the length of the guitar and the double bass (34 inches), was made of maple and screwed to the body. Sturdy Kluxon controls were required to cope with the tension of the four very thick strings. To help out any bass players who don't use a plectrum, there's a handy finger-rest under the last string. The single-coil pickup is divided in two with a magnet for each string. The volume and tone are controlled with a simple two-knob set-up. On the first Precisions, a chrome bridge cover (nicknamed the "ashtray") reduced the sustain and

helped produce a sound that was more similar to the warm, rounded sound of a double bass still demanded by jazz orchestras. Alongside this, Fender produced a 25-watt amplifier to cope with low frequencies. This Bassman, with its four speakers, went on to become incredibly popular.

The Precision went through some changes in 1954: its contours became more rounded and the headstock grew to resemble the Stratocaster. This is the most popular shape of the P-Bass and the one that we are most familiar with now, with a heavy, powerful sound that makes it the biggest-selling bass in the world.

Ovation

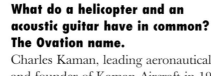

**What do a helicopter and an
acoustic guitar have in common?
The Ovation name.**

Charles Kaman, leading aeronautical engineer
and founder of Kaman Aircraft in 1945, was
also a talented guitar player. As a youngster,
he turned down an offer to play professionally
in Tommy Dorsey's prestigious orchestra, to
focus on his aeronautical studies. It was the
right choice: with his engineering degree in
the bag, he was involved in the early stages
of the helicopter industry. Then in 1956 his
company, which until then had specialised in
composite materials, began to diversify and
came up with a fibreglass folk guitar. His
engineers were experts in vibrations and
manufacturing materials and had the personal
inclination to test his instruments out. The
major innovation was the round back, which
was made possible thanks to this synthetic
material that could be moulded into any shape.
It was scientifically proven that the smooth
curves made the air circulate better; the
finished product resembled the guitar's
ancestor, the lute.

Jazz musician and bossa nova king Charlie
Byrd was one of the first to get excited
about it, saying that "it deserved an ovation!"
Kaman heard this, and decided it was the
perfect name.
In 1966, the first guitar made from
synthetic material came on the market with
an unexpected boost when well-known
country singer, Glen Campbell chose it for
his televised shows, which were seen by
millions of Americans every week.
The inspiration from aviation didn't stop
there. In 1970, Ovation developed the electric
acoustic pickup, the famous "piezo", which
reacts to the mechanical movement of the
strings and the sound board. Nicknamed the
Transducer, it was an attempt to get back to
the sound of an acoustic instrument unlike a
standard electric guitar pickup, which picks
up the vibrations of the strings in a magnetic
field. The first model fitted with these pickups
was the Balladeer with which, as the name
suggests, acoustic guitarists could move around
on stage, like a helicopter if they really wanted!

Ovation Adamas

In 1976 there was yet another innovation from
the Ovation's engineers, with the beautifully
crafted Adamas rounded fibreglass back.
After creating the rounded fibreglass back, the
engineers started on a sound board made from
synthetic materials. It needed to very thin, so
that it would vibrate properly, but also sturdy
enough to support the tension of the strings.
The material that they chose was carbon fibre,
with a similar grain to that of wood, which is
as hard as steel and lighter than aluminium.

That's where the name Adamas came
from: Latin for diamond, the indestructible
stone resulting from the transformation of
pure carbon.
A little acoustic jewel that cost over a
million dollars to develop. Of the 26 prototypes
that were built, number 19 ended up in the
hands of French guitarist, Marcel Dadi, who
recorded his album "Dadi à Nashville" on it,
with Chet Atkins' blessing.

Guitar Heroes

Marcel Dadi's career was closely linked to Ovation guitars from 1973 onwards: unashamedly modern, they were perfectly suited to his finger-picking style, and the rounded shape made it more comfortable to be played sitting down. It took just one meeting with Charles Kaman for the French guitarist to become the company's official face in France. He was closely involved in the design of the Adamas, which corresponded with his vision of the perfect guitar. A wide neck and the purest possible sound gave him the ideal opportunity to show off his breathtaking talent. Born in Tunisia in 1951, Marcel Dadi was the virtuoso guitarist who inspired thousands of youngsters to pick up a guitar in 1970s France. His famous *Méthode à Dadi* sold hundreds of thousands of copies. Every month, he released new tablatures in *Rock & Folk*.

He even recorded a series of lessons for TV. At the same time his educational activities, Marcel – who had a wicked sense of humour – opened a music shop in Paris, selling the latest imports from the States and Canada, where he often played with the grand masters of picking like Chet Atkins, who regarded him as a true country genius. It was as he was travelling back from one of these trips, after being honoured by the Nashville Country Music Hall of Fame, that he was killed in a plane crash on 17th July 1996.

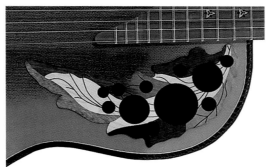

DEFINITIVE TRACKS

Galveston	**Glen Campbell**
Le derviche tourneur	**Marcel Dadi**
Swingy Boogie	**Marcel Dadi**
L'echo des savanes	**Marcel Dadi**

TRADE SECRETS

Every Adamas is tested in the laboratory to balance the sound and set the pieces in their definitive positions,

after which they won't budge, and there's nothing to fear from humidity or changes in temperature. The rounded sound box is moulded from a resin and synthetic fibre composite (lyrachord). The sound board reverberates like a drum, so the traditional central sound hole was no longer suitable. The designers decided to divide the airway into 11 different sized holes, on either side, close to the neck. They are integrated into carefully crafted wood from different species, representing stylised dead leaves, giving a camouflage effect. The headstock continues the theme of vegetation, as does the walnut

bridge which houses the six-pole piezo pickup developed by Ovation. It is linked up to an integrated preamplifier which is controlled by two volume and tone knobs on the top.

The original black carbon body made the Adamas look a bit austere, but it couldn't be varnished without the risk of changes to the sound. The solution was to shower it with glitter, making it shimmer like the diamond after which it was named.

Rickenbacker

Rickenbacker is often cited, and rightly so, as a pioneer when it comes to amplification. It was actually also one of the first companies to enjoy any success with electric instruments.

Born in Switzerland in 1886, Adolph Rickenbacher anglicised his name to Rickenbacker when he came to Los Angeles in 1920: in the business world, it was best to avoid any Germanic connotations in the period immediately following the First World War… After working as a steel supplier for the resonator guitar company, National, he developed an interest in the growing industry of amplified music. In 1931, he founded the Electro String Instrument Corporation with George Beauchamp, who was an inventor and lap steel guitar player. Together, they developed a horseshoe-shaped pickup which sensed the vibrations of the metal strings and transformed them into electrical impulses. Early prototypes were nicknamed Frying Pans because of their round bodies and long necks. But this was no novelty guitar: this electric steel instrument is regarded as the very first solid body with a magnetic pickup. The first models were called Electros, before becoming Rickenbacker Electros in 1934.

Rickenbacker's invention was not an immediate hit with the jazz or country scene, but the pickup worked and was a great success on Hawaiian guitars, which were enjoying considerable success in the inter-war years. The genre's biggest star Sol Hoopii, nicknamed The King of Steel Guitar, recorded his hit album, *Hula Blues* on a Rickenbacker.

The 1950s was the beginning of a new era for all guitar manufacturers. The arrival of rhythm and blues and "blues shouters" – the elder brothers of rock 'n' roll – dealt a fatal blow for lap steel guitars. George Beauchamp retired from the business, and in 1953, a disillusioned Adolph Rickenbacker sold his company to Francis C. Hall, an expert in distribution after working for Fender for some years. In 1956, Rickenbacker's 25th anniversary provided the perfect opportunity to revitalise the catalogue with a brand new design: the Combo 400, a semi-acoustic guitar with a central neck running right through the length of the guitar, which became the company's trademark. Designer Roger Rossmeisl came along in 1958, bringing with him the idea for the 300 series, popularised by John Lennon, who had bought his first Rickenbacker in Hamburg. The Fab Four became huge fans of the six- and 12-string models – and even the bass – which led to massive sales and resulted in the nickname Beatles-backers!

Rickenbacker's popularity has remained intact, but you'll have to wait around 12 months for your guitar: they are still made entirely by hand, according to traditional methods, in the Santa Ana factory in California. Rickenbacker is now the biggest manufacturer of guitars in the United States as other companies have outsourced production overseas.

The price tag might be a bit high for some, but as The Who's Pete Townshend said, if you're going to smash up a guitar, you might as well smash up an expensive one!

Rickenbacker 350V63 Jetglo.

Rickenbacker 300 series

Rickenbacker 330 Fireglo.

The 1958 Capri model defined Rickenbacker's direction since its takeover by F.C. Hall so well, that it was carried through with the famous 300 series.

Its ultra-modern look was created by German designer Roger Rossmeisl and firmly positioned Rickenbacker in the Pantheon of great American design. Its sound could be described as "ringing", with crystal-clear high notes that were all the rage in the 1960s, but which actually contributed to their decline when that same clear sound was no longer the in thing.

It epitomises the British Invasion led by The Beatles, followed by the amphetamine-fuelled Mod movement led by The Who's generation, revived in 1977 with a punk twist thanks to Paul Weller and The Jam. In the United States, "Rics" were the instrument of choice for the folk-rock revival of The Byrds and their descendents, from Tom Petty to Peter Buck (R.E.M.). With a more saturated sound, the Rickenbacker could hold its own with the likes of Steppenwolf's John Kay, who played *Born to Be Wild* on a legendary 381, which went on to become his signature model.

Rickenbacker 325C58 Jetglo – John Lennon.

DEFINITIVE TRACKS

Twist and Shout	The Beatles
Help	The Beatles
The One I Love	R.E.M.
A Town Called Malice	The Jam
American Girl	Tom Petty

Guitar Heroes

John Lennon's most famous guitar was the Rickenbacker Capri 325, which he bought the first time The Beatles went to Hamburg in 1960. An incredibly rare model designed two years before, with a hollow body with no f-holes and a natural finish. When he went back to Liverpool to play at The Cavern, John started using a Bigsby tremolo which was a great success, when he had no technical expertise at all. He went on to make other adjustments, the most noticeable of which was to paint it black, like George's Gretsch Duo Jet, to create a striking look… Plugged into a Vox AC30, the Capri 325 was the ultimate Mersey Beat guitar; it epitomised the early years of the Fab Four's career. In 1964, Rickenbacker started to make a special model for them, with an f-hole, a shorter neck and a tremolo arm.

In 1972, after The Beatles split up, John had his worn old Rickenbacker restored. He used it a lot on his last album, "Double Fantasy", as well as on the last song that he ever recorded, the track that was dedicated to Yoko Ono, *Walking on Thin Ice*, on 8th December 1980, just hours before he was assassinated in front of the Dakota Building in New York.

© Ebet Roberts/DALLE

Peter Buck, guitarist with R.E.M., is a great fan of Rickenbackers. Starting out with the band in the early 1980s in Athens, Georgia, he rediscovered the joys of the clear sound favoured by The Byrds' Roger McGuinn to sustain and envelop Michael Stipe's labyrinthine melodies and obscure text: a revolutionary combination of pure American rock and new-wave sensibilities introduced by Joy Division and The Cure from the other side of the Atlantic. The Rickenbacker 360 JetGlo black, with its hologram sticker of a pin-up, is right at the heart of all of R.E.M.'s recordings – all 16 studio albums so far – which have created a new perspective of independent rock, and enjoyed critical and public acclaim. Always remaining faithful to Rickenbacker, Peter Buck has quite a collection, including a 360V64 Fireglo George Harrison model and a 370/12 Roger McGuinn Signature model with 12 strings.

Trade Secrets

Guitars in the 300 series are maple semi-acoustics with a double crescent-shaped cutaway. The size of the body is quite impressive, but its ergonomic German Curve makes it very easy to handle. Plus, it's not too heavy for a solid body. At one end, the tailpiece with its chrome R is not just for effect – it's actually used to keep the strings in place. The thin polished maple neck has a reputation for being a bit slippery along the 24 frets. All of the guitars in the 300 series have five potentiometers: two for the volume, two for the tone

and one blend pot specific to Rickenbacker to balance out the two pickups, which isn't always easy to adjust but crucial to control the sound.

There are three distinct groups in the 300 series: the models between 310 and 325 are the smaller ones, initially designed for learners. The 325, popularised by John Lennon, doesn't have an f-hole, but does have three pickups.

The 330 is decorated with a stylised Art Deco hole and two single-coil pickups: the bridge pickup for a strident

sound, and the neck one for rounder tones. With a third pickup, it's the 340.

The 360, as seen in The Beatles film *A Hard Day's Night*, is the deluxe model, with a carefully designed finish and a stereo output; its rounded edges make it more comfortable. You'll recognise it by the mother-of-pearl triangle on the inlays. The three-pickup model is the 370. Basically, the ultimate guitar series for fans of the authentic sound.

Rickenbacker 360/12

Rickenbacker 360/12
Fireglo – Beatles.

© Gruhn Guitars

The thing about a 12-string guitar is that it produces a natural chorus effect, created by the different timbre of the two strings. The bass strings are tuned an octave apart, and the trebles in unison to produce a clearer sound. 12-string acoustic guitars are commonly used in folk music by solo singers, to create a broader sound. It is said to have its origins in Mexico, but Southern blues musicians were big fans too, including the likes of Blind Willie McTell in the 1920s, the legendary Leadbelly and his mix of folk and blues and Kurt Cobain (Nirvana) used one for *Where Did You Sleep Last Night* (on the album "Unplugged in New York").

In 1963, in the full throes of the folk revival and in the wake of Bob Dylan, Joan Baez and Peter, Paul & Mary, Rickenbacker had the clever idea of creating the first electric 12-string model. Roger McGuinn, who bridged the gap between Bob Dylan's folk and The Beatles' pop music, used a 360/12 to arrange a new version of *Mr. Tambourine Man* with The Byrds. Nothing was ever the same in the 1960s pop world...

Rickenbacker 360/12 Mapleglo.

DEFINITIVE TRACKS

Hard Day's Night	The Beatles
Mr. Tambourine Man	The Byrds

Guitar Heroes

In 1963, six months before the others, **George Harrison** was the first member of The Beatles to set foot on American soil. He went to visit his sister, incognito. Nobody had heard of the Fab Four on that side of the Atlantic. But after the band appeared on *The Ed Sullivan Show* in February 1964, all of that changed: they were an overnight sensation. George was soon approached by Rickenbacker, who offered him a 12-string electric guitar for a bit of an experiment.

During filming for the film *A Hard Day's Night*, the one they called "the quiet Beatle" was more than happy to flaunt it. The album of the same name, bridging the gap between folk and rock, struck a chord: Harrison's 12-string chord to be precise. Other Rickenbacker models, plus a sitar, can all be heard on the brilliant albums "Rubber Soul" and "Revolver", which led The Beatles into their new experimental era.

According to **Roger McGuinn**, The Byrds' sound would not have been possible if it wasn't for Rickenbacker's 12-string guitar. On a recommendation from Miles Davis and following in the Fab Four's wake, the folk-rock pioneers signed with Columbia in 1964. They dreamed of bringing together the worlds of Bob Dylan and The Beatles.

When they were played *Mr. Tambourine Man*, before it was released by Bob Dylan, their producer, Terry Melcher suggested that they produce a rock version. Roger McGuinn had the idea of using the famous electric 12-string guitar played by his hero George Harrison in the film *A Hard Day's Night*.

Rickenbacker 370/12 – Byrds.

The result exceeded all expectations and went to number one in record time. They were soon producing a string of Acid-tinged hits like *Turn, Turn, Turn* and *Eight Miles High*; they were on their way, and until 1968, nothing could stop them.

The Byrds were pioneering in many ways: after they launched folk rock and psychedelic rock, after persuading Dylan to go electric, Roger McGuinn – with a helping hand from Gram Parsons – invented country rock with the album "Sweetheart of the Rodeo". The jingle-jangle sound of the 12-string guitar made a comeback in the 1980s: after Tom Petty and R.E.M. came bands like The Plimsouls, The Replacements, The Church and The Jayhawks, all playing brilliant ringing Rickenbackers.

TRADE SECRETS

The Rickenbacker 360/12 was the first electric 12-string guitar. To look at, it's similar to the standard 360 model. The neck is the same, with the string doubles very close together, making it quite a challenge to get your fingers in the right place. Rickenbacker created an innovative new headstock to make room for all 12 strings without being too big. The tuners are on both sides as normal while the tuner posts project out at a right angle, making it look like a traditional guitar without too much distortion. As George Harrison raved, it's "the only 12 string you can change a string on when you're drunk". And he knew what he was talking about, as he was the proud owner of the second prototype which was

given to him as a gift by the manufacturer (another was given to country singer Suzy Arden). He tried it out when he was recording the album "A Hard Day's Night". It was a success, and so production could begin in 1964. Three models were introduced: the 360/12 with two single-coil pickups like George's, the 370/12 with three pickups like Roger McGuinn's from The Byrds, and the solid body 450/12 with two pickups.

The ringing Rickenbacker sound is thus doubled up thanks to the 12 strings, producing an extraordinary sound, not a million miles away from the Indian sitar.

Rickenbacker Bass

Rickenbacker had been interested in amplifying basses since the 1930s, starting with the neck of a double bass plugged straight into an amp. Production stopped in 1940, but the idea of a central neck survived in the design for the first electric bass. Unlike other manufacturers who went for screwed or glued necks, Rickenbacker chose a neck that extended throughout the length of the body. Its power and sturdiness were stressed in the 1957 catalogue, but it was the sustain produced by the neck design that would define the characteristic sound of this guitar. The result was enhanced by the use of a plectrum to produce clear, neat notes, which would make the bass such a crucial element in rock music.

In 1964, Rickenbacker offered Paul McCartney a left-handed 4001 S bass. It was heavier than his trusted Höfner, but he did start to use it in the studio in 1966 to record "Revolver" and of course, the "Sgt. Pepper" album. With that kind of endorsement, it soon became the favoured bass for 1970s progressive and experimental rock, played by Chris Squire from Yes, Mike Rutherford from Genesis and Roger Waters from Pink Floyd.

Rickenbacker Bass 4001C64S – McCartney.

Rickenbacker Bass 4001C64.

DEFINITIVE TRACKS

Close to the Edge	Yes
Owner of a Lonely Heart	Yes
Ace of Spades	Motörhead
Got to Get You into My Life	The Beatles

BASS HEROES

In 1965, four British bassists ordered a Rickenbacker bass from America. Founder member of Yes **Chris Squire**, was one of them. He started playing the bass after a bad acid trip which left him holed up at home for weeks with nothing but this instrument for company. Equipped with his 4001 bass, souped up with various effects from the wah-wah pedal to the tremolo arm, he was the only member of the band to appear on every single album released by Yes from the very beginning right through to the present day. The line-up has changed over the years, but the group was a leading light for prog rock in the 1970s when it released a number of concept albums which included tracks lasting for up to 20 minutes. Along with drummer Bill Briford, Chris Squire provided one of the most complex bass lines the genre has ever seen. Their mind-blowing arrangements really excel in their 1972 album, "Close to the Edge", which is generally regarded as the highpoint of their career, even though their commercial zenith came in 1983 with the more conventional pop hit *Owner of a Lonely Heart* produced with a helping hand from Trevor Horn (Buggles, Frankie Goes To Hollywood, etc.).

Lemmy Kilmister formed Motörhead in July 1975, after being chucked out of space rock band, Hawkwind for favouring amphetamines over his bandmate's preference for acid, despite the fact that he had contributed their biggest hit three years earlier: *Silver Machine*. With his Rickenbacker 4001 bass, Lemmy founded the ultimate rock 'n' roll band, adored by punk fans and heavy metal fans alike.

In 1979, following the release of the 4003, he plugged his bass into the stereo output of two Marshall Superbass 100-watt amps (nicknamed Murder One and Killer, and positioned on either side of the drummer). By his own admission, Lemmy plays "louder than anyone else", with a style that sounds like a combination of a rhythm guitar, a bass and an earthquake all at the same time. As well as being loud, the music is played at a breakneck speed, with the drummer playing a bass drum and the guitarist forbidden from playing solos. Listen to "Bomber", "Overkill" or "Ace of Spaces", the trio of albums which launched Motörhead's career. To find out more about his lifestyle of sex, drugs and rock 'n' roll, read his eye-opening and hilarious autobiography, *White Line Fever* – the title needs no explanation.

© Clausel/DALLE

Lemmy Kilmister.

Rickenbacker Bass 4001CS Chris Squire.

Rickenbacker Bass 4004LK Lemmy Kilmister.

TRADE SECRETS

All Rickenbacker basses are still carefully crafted in the United States in Santa Ana, and production methods haven't really changed. The most recognisable is the extravagantly curved 4000, designed by luthier Roger Rossmeisl in 1957. It's a balanced design, and relatively light despite the prominent horn and the maple fins attached to the central neck. This neck is slim and fast, with a 20-fret rosewood fingerboard. This is extended with a headstock made in the same style as the body. Towards the end of the 1950s, the first series were fitted with Rickenbacker's famous horseshoe pickups which wrapped around all of the strings.

1961 saw the release of the 4001 which was destined to become the most successful model with its two identical pickups on the neck and the bridge, and a fairly imposing capo. The volume and tone could be adjusted on either pickup.

On the 4003, launched in 1979, the stereo output (Ric-O-Sound) meant that the signal could be sent to two different amps: the lower neck pickup was hooked up to the bass amp, and the higher bridge pickup, used for saturation, went to the guitar amp. And there you have the secret to Lemmy's success and to Motörhead's phenomenal power!

Taylor

The history of the Taylor name started relatively recently. It all began in 1973 in Lemon Grove, California, when two young students met: Bob Taylor and Kurt Listug. Both passionate musicians, they started to learn how to make guitars at American Dream, Sam Radding's little guitar-making shop, just over the road from campus. Barely one year later, Taylor and Listug joined forces with Steve Schemmer to buy American Dream, which they immediately renamed Westland Music Company. It was Taylor's name that stuck, both because it sounded good and because it was concise enough to appear as a logo on the guitars designed by Bob, who was the trio's real guitar craftsman, while Listug took care of the business side of things. Founded in 1974, the company has continued to grow ever since, and now employs some 450 people. Ranging from good quality to top-of-the-range, Taylor guitars are distributed around the world.

Taylor 814-CE.

The first guitar produced by Bob Taylor, when he was just 17 years old, had 12 strings. He retained a soft spot for the 12-string model and included one in every series he produced, classed according to quality: from 100 for the lower-end versions up to 900 for deluxe models.

Neil Young was one of the first major names to fall for a 12-string Taylor 855, as seen in the 1979 film, *Rust Never Sleeps*. He has taken one on tour with him ever since.

In the mid-1980s, when synthetic pop filled the charts, guitar makers were not enjoying the blues, and acoustic music didn't get a look-in in the videos that were being played on MTV. But Taylor relished a challenge, and created a model for Prince. "Purple Rain" was the name of the game, and the brand-new superstar ordered himself a purple 12-string 655. Despite the fact that he had refused to play an instrument with visible branding brand could be seen, the deal was done.

The list of musicians playing a Taylor today is quite impressive: Aerosmith, Dave Grohl (Foo Fighters), Billy Corgan (Smashing Pumpkins), Suzanne Vega, Pearl Jam, Lucinda Williams, Lenny Kravitz, Beck, The Pretenders, R.E.M., Mick Jagger, Alanis Morissette, Joe Satriani, Mark Knopfler, The Edge, Steve Vai... need I go on?

Taylor GA4-12 (12 strings).

DEFINITIVE TRACKS

Constant Craving	k.d. lang
Living in the Country	Leo Kottke
4 the Tears in Your Eyes	Prince

Guitar Heroes

As a young singer and guitarist, Canadian musician Kathryn Dawn Lang was prepared to pay the high price for an acoustic 550, and wrote her first country folk songs on it. She's now better known as **k.d. lang**, but she and her guitar are still inseparable.

This outspoken artist, who has not been given an easy ride on the traditionalist country music scene (when she came out, or when she announced that she was a vegetarian – not the most popular thing to be in her cattle-ranching homeland), has nevertheless had an incredibly successful career, including four Grammy awards thanks to her extraordinary vocal range and her incredibly poignant writing.

Guitar virtuoso **Leo Kottke** has always had close links with the Taylor family. Since 1990, Bob Taylor has been making customised signature acoustic models for him, with either six or 12 strings. His energetic finger-picking technique is breathtaking. Despite a burst eardrum caused by a firework when he was a child, Leo Kottke has enjoyed immense success ever since his first album, "6 and 12 String" was released in 1969. His vigorous playing technique has caused him a few problems with tendonitis, so he slowed down a bit and adopted a more traditional playing style, before returning to his favoured 12-string guitar, encouraged by his biggest fan and admirer, Bob Taylor himself.

© Martin Philbey-Redferns/DALLE

k.d. lang.

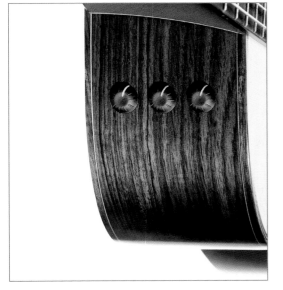

TRADE SECRETS

Bob Taylor concentrated his efforts on guitars with a flat sound board and steel strings. He took such care in his craft and in the sound of the finished product that word of mouth quickly secured the good reputation of his guitars. Thanks to a number of innovations, including the bolt-on neck and the glued-on headstock, he was able to mass-produce very good quality, sturdy low-end models with a sound that blew the competition out of the water. The 100 series, made from good-quality wood varieties, is the perfect example. At the opposite end of the range, the catalogue had the prestigious line of Taylor Presentations, which were made using very rare wood species, like Brazilian rosewood which is highly valued by guitar makers and now a protected species. Each guitar is made individually, and finished with meticulous care and craftsmanship.

Surprisingly, one of the most popular Taylor models is the Baby, a very basic model originally for learners, which has reinvented itself as a handy and effective travel guitar. It's now commonly seen on stage and in the studio, rubbing shoulders with its older sister. Since 2003, electric acoustic models have been fitted with the patented incorporated preamp – the Taylor Expression System – which retains the nuanced sounds of an amplified acoustic guitar without any distortion.

PRS – Paul Reed Smith

The small company started by Paul Reed Smith, PRS Guitars, has quickly earned quite a reputation in the modern guitar world. Its electric models take the best features of Gibsons and Fenders to produce guitars for the most demanding players, as long as their wallets can cope with it.

PRS – Private Stock Carlos Santana II.

Paul Reed Smith has been a huge guitar fan all his life. He produced his first guitar, a 12 string, in 1976, as a challenge for his university studies. He came top in the assignment. Over the next ten years, at the rate of one guitar a month, Paul gradually grew his business by selling his instruments to passing musicians with an irresistible offer: he promised to give them their money back if they didn't fall in love with their purchase. His daring gamble paid off, and his happy customers included Ted Nugent, Al Di Meola, Carlos Santana and Peter Frampton. Confident in his abilities, in 1985, P.R. Smith founded his own company with the firm intention of making only the best guitars using only the best materials. Serious about his intentions, he sought advice from Ted McCarty, Gibson's boss in its golden age of Les Pauls, SGs, Explorers and Flying Vs. The prestigious consultant gave him all his trade secrets on a plate. PRS is now based in Stevensville (Maryland) and employs 120 people making 41 guitars a day. Their output includes the little jewels referred to by the boss as Private Stock Guitars, as a nod to the unique individual models he made when he was starting out. His passion has certainly paid off!

DEFINITIVE TRACKS

Put Your Lights On	Santana
Migra	Santana

Guitar Heroes

On stage at Woodstock in August 1969, Santana had everybody on their feet with *Soul Sacrifice* and its Latin beat combined with the legendary sustain of a Gibson SG. Mexican-born **Carlos Santana** was the first rock star to play what we now know as world music: his mix of salsa and guitar genius enjoyed immediate success with hits like the Fleetwood Mac cover, *Black Magic Woman* and *Oye Como Va* (by Tito Puente). Keen to get involved in any musical experience, Santana flirted with jazz rock on a Les Paul, which held its own next to John McLaughlin, Herbie Hancock and Wayne Shorter. In the mid-1970s, influenced by guru Sri Chinmoy, Carlos changed his name: Devadip (the light of God's lamp) started playing a top-of-the-range Yamaha SG2000, which demonstrated his high standards as well as his desire to get out of his comfort zone. In 1985, he readopted his original name, and Carlos Santana discovered a young guitar maker who used to wait for him after his concerts to offer him his home-made guitars. He willingly had a go on a Paul Reed Smith: he tried one, then two, then three, then four…

was he dreaming? These brilliantly crafted guitars were exactly what he needed. He and his PRSs were soon inseparable. The guitar legend with 50 million album sales under his belt and an instantly recognisable style has nothing left to prove. Not that that stopped him kicking off the millennium with "Supernatural", which won him two Grammy Awards (one for best album of the year, the other for best rock album).

With PRS guitars, we enter the realms of haute couture: the craftsmanship and attention to detail are second to none. The great thing about a PRS is its perfect sustain, even on the farthest frets, like a Gibson, and a reliable tremolo arm like a Fender.

TRADE SECRETS

A lethal weapon with an ultra-clean sound, particularly well suited to jazz or any kind of music that requires any sort of finesse. But these highly adaptable instruments can also handle the demands of a bigger sound, and have become popular with bands like Linkin Park and Limp Bizkit on the neometal scene. Not to mention Dave Navarro, former guitarist with Jane's Addiction and the Red Hot Chili Peppers, and now with Panic Channel, who has been playing a PRS since 1987. He now even has his very own signature model, nicknamed the Jet White. Carlos Santana tried various PRS models over a decade or so before agreeing to one being marketed with his name attached to it. He now has a number of signature models, of varying quality, including his favourite guitar, the Santana II. Unable to believe his ears or his

fingers, Santana called his PRSs an "accident of God". A mahogany body with a similar shape to that of a Les Paul, finished off with a flame maple top, a mahogany neck covered in a 24-fret rosewood fingerboard with the famous soaring eagle inlays, optimum access to the high notes thanks to the cutaway hollowed out from the body and a tremolo arm with a very reliable locking mechanism. When it comes to pickups, there are two special humbuckers (Santana Zebra Coil) to get the thick sound with excellent saturation.
PRS paid Carlos for the right to use his name which funds charity work in Tijuana.

Dobro

The word Dobro has entered into the language to describe resonator guitars: it's also first and foremost a brand created by the Dopyera brothers, who were originally from a large family of musicians in Eastern Europe who specialised in traditional folk violins and came to the United States at the beginning of the 20th century.
They initially founded the National company and invented the resonator guitar. In 1930, the five brothers, John, Robert, Rudolph, Louis and Emil, founded Dobro, short for Dopyera Brothers.
When they left National, the Dopyera brothers lost the right to use the resonator name, so they submitted a second patent application for an inverted star-shaped resonator called the Spider, more commonly used on wood-bodied guitars.

Dobro and National often get muddled up. To keep things simple, we could say that a National is a steel guitar commonly used with a bottleneck to play the blues (see the chapter on National), while Dobros are wooden guitars with a metal resonator. This new instrument, similar to the lap steel guitar, was quickly adopted by bluegrass and country musicians.
After all of the Dopyera brothers had passed away, the Dobro name was bought by Gibson in 1993, and has used the brand name ever since. New Dobro models are made according to traditional methods in workshops in Nashville, Tennessee.

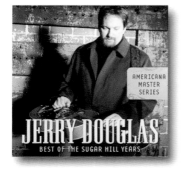

DEFINITIVE TRACKS

Birdland	Jerry Douglas
Lonesome Dobro	Tut Taylor
The Ballad of Curtis Lowe	Lynyrd Skynyrd
When Papa Played the Dobro	Johnny Cash

© Jeff Moore-Zuma/DALLE

The master of the modern Dobro is **Jerry Douglas**: he can be heard on over 2,000 albums, playing in all sorts of different styles, with artists as diverse as Paul Simon, Ray Charles, James Taylor and Lyle Lovett, as well as on the soundtrack of *O Brother, Where Art Thou?*, which sold more than 8 million copies.

John Fogerty has also had a prolific guitar, rewarded with a whopping 11 Grammy awards! Famous for his traditional slide technique, he got interested in Dobro guitars as a teenager. He now plays a Beard or a Scheerhorn: in other words, the best resonator guitars on the market. Since 1988, Jerry

Douglas has been a member of Union Station, the group that accompanies country singer and violinist Alison Krauss, who herself holds the record for the number of Grammy Awards won by a female artist, with 20 in her collection so far!

TRADE SECRETS

With its spider resonator, Dobro is perfect for bluegrass. It is played flat, with a metal slide on a square neck, or like a normal guitar with a round neck. Dobro players only use heavy-gauge strings to make sure the resonators really vibrate, usually up to 18–56 for sliding. Experts say that they rarely last for more than 25 hours before they are worn down by the sliding technique. A new cone resonator guitar needs to be broken in for a good number of hours to achieve the right sound. On the other end of the scale, cones are worn down over time, so they need to be replaced to maintain the ideal clarity. In theory, a Dobro doesn't need to be amplified – this is

why it was invented – but to produce a sound to fill large venues, there are special pickups which should be used with care: feedback and untimely vibrations from the resonator are a risk.

To hear a genuine country Dobro sound, listen to Lynyrd Skynyrd's *The Ballad of Curtis Lowe* or Johnny Cash's *When Papa Played the Dobro*. For a comprehensive experience, see if you can get your hands on "The Great Dobro Sessions", a compilation of bluegrass and country giants including Jerry Douglas, Tut Taylor, Mike Auldridge, Curtis Burch and many more.

National

National was set up in the 1920s by the Dopyera brothers who went on to found Dobro. The two labels merged in 1932 and became the National Dobro Company. By the 1950s, the resonator guitar was struggling to keep up with the times, and was starting to be regarded as a relic from a bygone age, only to be found in the hands of a collector or a blues aesthete like Johnny Winter or the Allman Brothers Band in the 1970s.

Everything changed the following decade when Dire Straits' classic , "Brothers in Arms" (with a National Style O on the cover) came out at almost exactly the same time as Ry Cooder's soundtrack for *Paris Texas* was released, bringing the slide guitar back into fashion. These two events inspired passionate guitar makers Don Young and McGregor Gaines to buy National and give the steel guitar a new lease of life with the National Reso-Phonic. Building on the foundations of this legendary name, they came up with brand new models without losing the authentic feel of these roots guitars, which were tried and tested by the brilliant Bob Brozman.

Since the 1990s, the patent for the resonator system has come into the public domain, so lots of companies have started producing these metal guitars offering their products, of varying quality, to a broad audience.

THE STEEL GUITAR

The whole history of modern music can be looked at against a backdrop of the quest for volume. So that guitars can be heard in jazz orchestras or on street corners, ingenious new amplification methods needed to be found. And so the steel guitar was born, fitted with a metal resonator and always used with a slide.

The classic way of playing is to slide a "bottleneck" along the strings. This method was introduced in Hawaii in the 19th century with a Kika guitar resting on the player's lap. It soon travelled to the Southern States, with the migration of black musicians.

In early 1920s Los Angeles, the Dopyera brothers, sons of Eastern European immigrants, and George Beauchamp (future cofounder of Rickenbacker) invented the resonator system. They used it on a guitar made entirely of steel with a square neck to be played flat, as in the Hawaiian method. The name National was nothing to do with their patriotism: it was a reference to the sports car of the same name produced by Chrysler.

Guitar Heroes

Historian, collector and talented musician, **Bob Brozman** is the greatest slide guitar expert around. Born in New York in 1954, he has been playing the guitar since he was six years old, and discovered the joys of the National steel guitar when he was 13. At university he studied ethnomusicology and became an expert in the subject, publishing books about Hawaiian music, collecting old blues 78s and in 1980, he started recording his own albums. With his astonishing technique, Brozman has tackled all sorts of music – jazz, blues, calypso etc. – taking his National steel guitar around the world with him. His albums boast some brilliant collaborations with musicians from all four corners of the world, including India, Africa, Asia and Europe.

DEFINITIVE TRACKS

Death Letter	**Son House**
Dust My Broom	**Elmore James**
Romeo and Juliette	**Dire Straits**
Devil Got My Woman	**Bob Brozman**

TRADE SECRETS

The resonator system invented by Dopyera amplified the sound mechanically with a lightweight cone made of an aluminium alloy. The vibration of the strings is retransmitted via the instrument to the cone, which works as a sort of loud speaker. Early models had three cones positioned in a triangle formation, which is where the name Tricone came from, commonly used in Hawaiian music. In the 1930s, for financial reasons, the process was modified to work with a larger single cone using a wooden "biscuit", often associated with the Delta blues. As with chrome guitars, the shimmering body is made entirely of steel, with Hawaiian palm trees engraved on the back. Nickel bronze, brass and copper are also used, but the sound was the same: it is only the resonator that had an effect on the sound.

The round neck is of course made of wood, in this case, maple with a 14-fret ebony fingerboard. It wasn't just a guitar, it was a work of art!

Thanks to Alan Lomax, the first musicologist to record musicians from the Mississippi delta, the birthplace of the blues, in the 1920s and 1930s, the poignant songs of Son House (*Death Letter*), Charley Patton (*Pony Blues*), Skip James (*Devil Got My Woman*) and Elmore James (*Dust My Broom*) can still be enjoyed today. The original thrill of the slide guitar played on indestructible Nationals.

Epiphone

Epiphone has considerable experience producing stringed instruments and has been a true pioneer in the field. The story dates back to 1870, with Anastasios Stathopoulo, a Greek craftsman making lutes, bouzoukis and flutes who lived in Turkey until tensions between the countries at the beginning of the 20th century compelled the family to emigrate to America.
Working from a modest workshop in Manhattan, Stathopoulo and his family started to make use of their expertise to make mandolins, which were incredibly fashionable at the time. After the death of his father in 1915, the workshop was taken over by Epaminondas, known as Epi to his friends. He grew the family business by turning his attention to the banjo with the Epiphone Banjo Corporation.
Aware that times were changing, Epiphone (literally "the voice of Epi") released its first guitar in 1929. With names like Broadway, Triumph and Royal, it's easy to recognise the Gibson L-5's influence on the first series.

Competition was fierce, and Epiphone didn't shy away from using a picture of a naked lady in an advertising campaign to sell the merits of the Emperor, an impressive response to Gibson's Super 400. Despite continuing support from jazz musicians, the company never recovered from Epi's death in 1943. His brothers, Orphie and Frixo, had to deal with a difficult economic environment and waves of strikes. Epiphone eventually sold out to Gibson in 1957 for the modest sum of $20,000. A new era began for the brand with a new home in Kalamazoo, Gibson's legendary base. 1964 saw the release of two new models, the Sheraton and the Casino which were miraculously adopted by The Beatles. A decline in business in the 1970s saw further decentralisation: Epiphone guitars were made in Japan, then Korea, and finally in China. With its mass-produced output, Epiphones are now seen as a catalogue of cheap Gibson copies, recommended only for absolute beginners.

Epiphone Casino

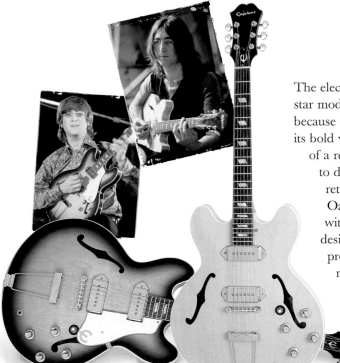

The electric acoustic Casino, one of Epiphone's star models, is still popular with collectors because of John Lennon's passion for it. With its bold vintage look and the reasonable price of a reissue (from under £500), it continues to delight brit-pop fans today and its return to popularity was helped by Oasis with the Supernova emblazoned with the Union Jack. It is specifically designed to be played as a backing guitar providing a warm, clear sound, but not recommended for solos because access to anything above the 12th fret is not easy.
It's interesting that the Casino, based on a low-end guitar for beginners, was more

successful than the one that it copied, the Gibson ES-330. That has to be down to the fact that The Beatles, The Rolling Stones and The Kinks all used Casinos in their backline because they were fairly cheap and so could be handled without much care and attention on stage!

Epiphone
performance is our passion

Guitar Heroes

Epiphone John Lennon 1965 Casino.

Epiphone John Lennon Revolution Casino.

Epiphone Supernova (Oasis).

In the 1960s, anything that had anything to do with The Beatles was considered sacred. Every new instrument that appeared with the group created a huge stir for the manufacturers and guaranteed a rise in sales.

In 1964, **Paul McCartney** was the first to get his hands on an Epiphone. His first were the Texan acoustic which he used (and still uses) to play *Yesterday* live, and a left-handed Casino. Plugged into a Vox AC30 amp, this was what he used for the riff in *Paperback Writer* and the solo in *Taxman*.

George Harrison and **John Lennon** then both bought a Casino sunburst to record "Revolver" in 1966. Harrison's had a Bigsby tremolo.

During the psychedelic *Sgt. Pepper* era, Lennon had his Rolls and his piano painted by Dutch design collective, The Fool, and customised his Epiphone in white and grey. In contrast, for the double album "The Beatles" (White album) in 1968, he had it totally stripped to reveal the natural wood colour for a return to purity.

Epiphone rereleased Lennon's Casino in two different versions: the 1965 sunburst, and the one that's now known as the Revolution, with its stripped finish. This is what Lennon was playing in the videos for *Revolution* and *Hey Jude*, as well as during the famous rooftop concert on 30th January 1969 on top of the premises of their record label, Apple which was The Beatles' last concert and the culmination of shooting for the film *Let It Be*.

DEFINITIVE TRACKS

Paperback Writer	**The Beatles**
Revolution	**The Beatles**
Get Back	**The Beatles**

TRADE SECRETS

Epiphone Sheraton John Lee Hooker.

The Casino was produced in 1964, with a hollow, maple body. It works well as an acoustic guitar, but reaches its full potential when it's plugged into an amp (a Vox AC30). The two single-coil P-90 pickups give it its clear, vibrant sound, typical of the 1960s. The narrow neck is supposed to be very comfortable and is usually made of mahogany with a rosewood fingerboard. The Casino is instantly recognisable thanks to its trapeze tailpiece giving it a touch of jazz. Surprisingly light, thanks to its hollow body, you can feel it vibrate under the chords, with a tendency to produce some feedback which makes it seem as though the guitar is playing itself!

The Casino should not be muddled up with the Epiphone Sheraton favoured by John Lee Hooker, even though it has the same shape. This model is in fact a copy of the semi-acoustic Gibson ES-335 with a central solid block, guaranteeing more sustain and reducing feedback. It's also fitted with humbucker pickups.

Höfner

Historically, the company was founded in 1887 in Schönbach, by the brilliant luthier, Karl Höfner. Located in the heart of a region full of woods and forests, the company grew to become the biggest manufacturer of stringed instruments in Germany. Specialising of course in violins and cellos, when the business was passed on to its founder's sons, Josef and Walter in 1920, the catalogue started to include guitars.

After the Second World War, the Höfner family fled their home town, which was now part of East Germany and settled in Bubenreuth. In their new factory, they began producing excellent guitars, like the Golden Höfner, the President and the Committee, which became very popular with the jazz fraternity and are now highly collectable. In 1956 Walter Höfner invented the 500/1 bass, sometimes known as the violin bass. Paul McCartney bought one in the early years of The Beatles when he was in Hamburg, so when Beatlemania kicked in between 1963 and 1964, they soon became incredibly popular. As a result Höfner certainly deserves a place in guitar legend.

Violin Bass

Paul McCartney chose the violin bass for a number of reasons. The first was to do with cost: in Hamburg, where The Beatles were struggling to kick off their career in the early 1960s, Höfner basses were common and a lot cheaper than Fenders. He purchased his first for the modest sum of £30 – a real bargain for such a well-made instrument. Secondly, the violin bass is symmetrical, so it could easily be converted to a left-hand bass for Paul. In 1963, Paul got a second Höfner which he still uses today, both on stage and in the studio.

Höfner Bass Violin 500/1 Vintage 62 (McCartney).

Höfner Bass Violin 500/1 (50th anniversary 1956–2006).

DEFINITIVE TRACKS

I Saw Her Standing There	The Beatles
I Want to Hold Your Hand	The Beatles
Can't Buy Me Love	The Beatles

Guitar Heroes

Paul McCartney became The Beatles' bassist by default in April 1961 after Stuart Sutcliffe left and nobody else wanted the job: John had just bought his Rickenbacker and George clearly relished the role of soloist. At this time, The Beatles were based in Hamburg, and were set to record with producer Bert Kaempfert (the only man to have worked with The Beatles, Frank Sinatra and Elvis Presley!) to accompany Tony Sheridan on a number of tracks including *My Bonnie*.

This bass, which was as light as a normal guitar and easy to handle, gave Paul a great deal of freedom to move around on stage. The narrow neck enabled him to play the melodic bass lines which were so typical of his jazzy style. McCartney stopped playing the Höfner in 1966, when The Beatles stopped touring. Paul then chose the superior Rickenbacker bass and spent two intensely creative years holed up in the Abbey Road studio resulting in the release of "Revolver", "Sgt. Pepper's Lonely Hearts Club Band" and "The Beatles" (White album). The original legendary bass saw the light of day again on the roof of Apple in the cold wind of 30th January 1969, waving a final goodbye to The Beatles years.

After many long years in the wilderness, the violin bass has returned to become an integral

part of McCartney's modern sound. His faithful '63 Höfner has become the emblem for his recent tours, with each tour turning into the ultimate juke-box experience.

TRADE SECRETS

Introduced at the Frankfurt music show in 1956, the violin bass is a hollow body guitar without a sound hole, made of spruce and maple. Because of its resonance and floating bridge, it produces a velvety, warm sound. It bears a passing resemblance to the Gibson EB-1, Gibson's electric bass produced between 1953 and 1958, also shaped like a violin, but which did not enjoy anywhere near the same level of success.

The Contemporary Series includes models with original Höfner Staple Top pickups and have a central block of wood to increase the sustain and depth of the 500/1. Made in China, under German control, it is now possible to get hold one of Macca's genuine basses for well under £600. For the reissued 1963 vintage model, hand-made in Germany, you're looking at something over twice that, and to be honest, you can hardly tell the difference from a distance!

Selmer

The only French guitar to enjoy a great deal of international success, the Selmer is the jazz model used by Django Reinhardt. It was created by Italian guitar maker Mario Maccaferri in the early 1930s and produced in the Selmer workshops for just twenty years.

The founder, Henri Selmer, was a well-known clarinettist who started making reeds and clarinets in his Montmartre workshop in 1885.

The company grew in 1929 when it bought the workshop of Adolphe Sax who had invented the saxophone. From then on, Selmer's work focused on producing saxophones and the company soon became world-famous for this.

The company is still run by the Selmer family, and now employs 600 people in its historic base in Mantes-la-Ville (Yvelines). A large proportion of its wind instruments are exported, offering quality far superior to that of Asian competitors.

Selmer-Maccaferri Jazz

© Photothèque Henri Selmer

In 1932, Selmer welcomed Italian luthier Mario Maccaferri into its workshops. The passionate jazz and classical music fan had developed a resonator system to go inside the guitar. Between 1932 and 1934, he worked on the natural amplification of steel string guitars used on the booming jazz scene. The result was a model for orchestras called the Jazz, which went down well with improvisers and folk musicians. A misunderstanding between Maccaferri and Selmer ended their fruitful partnership after two years, but the guitar continued to be produced for the next 20 years, right through to 1952: only 900 copies ever came out of the workshop. The ultimate acoustic jazz guitar, the Selmer-Maccaferri was Django Reinhardt's instrument of choice throughout his career. Originals are incredibly rare but it has been reissued by excellent luthiers including Jacques Favino, who used to make guitars for the likes of Georges Brassens, and more recently, by Maurice Dupont who has carried on where Selmer left off.

© Photothèque Henri Selmer

DEFINITIVE TRACKS

Nuages	Django Reinhardt
Minor Swing	Django Reinhardt
Bossa Dorado	Trio Rosenberg
Daphné	Biréli Lagrène

Django Reinhardt and the Hot Club Quintet.

and couldn't spell out his own name to the producers of the recording. The same year, his caravan was destroyed by a fire, leaving his leg and left hand with serious burns and he lost the use of two fingers. He spent 18 months in hospital and had to relearn how to play the guitar that his brother Nin-Nin brought him. With incredible will power, he developed a method of playing using his good fingers and at the same time, he was discovering jazz and listening to 78s by Duke Ellington and Louis Armstrong. In the 1930s, Django founded a quintet called the Hot Club de France with violinist Stéphane Grappelli, which enjoyed international success. Of his hundreds of recordings, his rendition of *La Marseillaise* to celebrate the Liberation of France in 1945 has remained famous, as well his huge hit, *Nuages*. Django Reinhardt's heritage is immense, breaking out from music and restoring the travelling community's pride in their freedom.

A vast number of guitarists have been influenced by Django. Some of the most prominent include Biréli Lagrène, Angelo Debarre, and the Rosenberg Trio. He was one of the first to use a playing method which is now popularised by the likes of Sanseverino and Thomas Dutronc.

The greatest jazz guitarist of all time, **Django Reinhardt**, played Selmer guitars throughout his career. They suited his powerful style of play completely, offering a reassuring sturdiness that was perfect for his nomadic lifestyle. He invented gypsy jazz – traditional Romani music, brought up to date with his brilliant technique and a touch of swing inspired by American jazz. Django was born in a caravan on 23rd January 1910 to a family of travellers based in Belgium. He learned the banjo young, finding it disconcertingly easy. When he was 18, he recorded his first record using the name Jiango Renard: he was illiterate

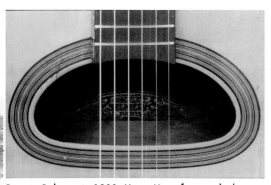

Born in Bologna in 1900, Mario Maccaferri studied with the Italian maestro, Mozzani. He applied the same techniques as for a traditional guitar on the jazz model,

TRADE SECRETS

adding personal touches like the cutaway – a novelty at the time. He also designed a rosewood floating bridge which lies on a solid spruce body along the same lines as for archtop guitars and mandolins. The back and the sides were made of Indian rosewood.

In 1931, Maccaferri applied for a patent for a resonator to naturally amplify the sound of the acoustic guitar. For this, he designed a sound box big enough to house a second resonator box under the sound hole. This first Selmer-Maccaferri guitar, used by Django when he was

starting out, had a D-shaped sound hole. It was particularly useful for providing a beat as it projected the sound in all directions. When Maccaferri left, Selmer removed the resonator and replaced it with a smaller O-shaped sound hole. This model, the "petite bouche" (small mouth) is the one that became best known. Django Reinhardt used it to develop his solo playing thanks to its more concentrated sound projection and clearer high notes.

Valco

In the 1940s, Valco was set up by former managers of the National Dobro Company. The company name is made up of the first name initials of its founders, Victor Smith, Al Frost and Louis Dopyera, plus "Co". For a long time, Valco made metal resonator guitars similar to National's before they launched the first plastic guitars in a range of bright colours in the 1950s. Models that collectors get excited about today include the

Supro Belmont and the National Val-Pro.
In 1967, Valco merged with Kay, which had been producing musical instruments since the 1930s. This partnership ended scarcely a year later, which put an end to the production of plastic guitars.

Valco
Airline 2P DLX
Jack White
(White Stripes).

Eastwood Res-O-Glas Airline

The fibreglass Airline Res-O-Glas guitars produced between 1958 and 1967 were reasonably priced guitars sold exclusively from a catalogue by Montgomery Ward, the first mail-order retail chain in the world.

It wasn't until the beginning of the 21st century and the success of The White Stripes, the famous two-tone phenomenon from Detroit, that people started taking Airline guitars seriously again. The original models, which cost next to nothing originally, are now prohibitively expensive and, it has to said, often unplayable.

Canadian Mike Robinson had the brilliant idea of making replicas with the Eastwood name. A comprehensive range including all of these 1960s guitars in all the colours of the rainbow is now produced in Korea: these decent guitars which produce a retro sound and an original look are sold for a very reasonable price.

Valco
Airline 3P DLX
Joey Burns
(Calexico).

DEFINITIVE TRACKS

Seven Nation Army	The White Stripes
Icky Thumb	The White Stripes
Too Much Alcohol	J. B. Hutto

Guitar Heroes

Jack White wasn't the first rock star to play one of these famous plastic guitars: **David Bowie** has a Supro Dual Tone and Calexico's **Joey Burns** regularly goes on stage with one of these slightly kitsch models. Jack names blues legend **J. B. Hutto** – the grand master of the slide guitar whose hit *Too Much Alcohol* has since been covered by Rory Gallagher – who used to play a scarlet Airline.

The White Stripes guitarist bought his first Airline for cash (just $200!) from Jack Yarber from the Oblivians, a garage band from Memphis, backstage after one of their gigs. It wasn't in a particularly good state, but Jack was seduced by the charms of his red guitar; his second Airline was a gift from a fan who had bought it on eBay for $3,000.

Success came to the band with the release of their album "Elephant" and the huge hit single *Seven Nation Army* with the best guitar riff since Nirvana's *Smells Like Teen Spirit.*

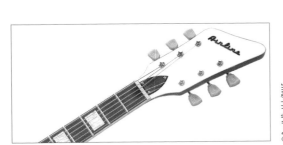

© Ross Halfin-Idols/DALLE

Jimmy Page & Jack White, 2005.

TRADE SECRETS

The 1960s Airline Res-O-Glas was made of two fibreglass plastic casts, covered in a thick coat of red paint. The two parts were attached to each other by a strip of white rubber which covered the solid wood section. The screw-on neck was made of maple with a rosewood fingerboard. There's a bit of a trick with the pickups: they are single-coils disguised as humbuckers. It has to

be said that accuracy isn't the strong point of the vintage models, but this seems to amuse The White Stripes guitarist, Jack White, who says that he likes it "when things are messed up… "

The Eastwood replicas are a lot more reliable, with two humbuckers on vintage Alnico magnets providing a high output level. The body is no longer fibreglass (Res-O-

Glas), but instead is covered with mahogany. It's still just as light because the body is hollow, with a reinforced structure. This is one of the secrets to the slightly cavernous sound of the new Airlines, with a greater depth and clarity. Eastwood models are easily recognisable thanks to the fact that the white plastic join around the guitar is no longer there.

Dean Guitars

Dean Guitars is an American brand founded in 1977 by Dean Zelinsky, a young music fanatic who was just 19 years old at the time. In just a few years, he was regarded as an expert in guitars with an aggressive look and a gut-wrenching sound: perfect for heavy metal!

He started to play the guitar when he was 10, at the same time as he developed an interest in his dad's DIY workshop. As a teenager, his studies let him work afternoons in his own guitar repair shop. He gradually began to design original instruments with one simple philosophy: to rival Gibson, taking inspiration from the Flying V and the Explorer. Quite a challenge!

Dean has revealed that after just two visits to Gibson's premises at Kalamazoo, he had taken enough notes to equip him with the tools to manufacture guitars in his factory in Evanston, Illinois. Aware that he would have to do a great deal to stand out from the competition, Dean made a name for himself with a sexy marketing strategy, asking *Playboy* models to strike suggestive and alluring poses to show off his guitars. This sexist use of women caused quite a stir, but it did raise Dean's profile among young, testosterone-pumped guitarists…

Paradoxically, early fans of Dean guitars were mainly serious musicians like Kerry Livgren from the band Kansas, and the Doobie Brothers, both big in the 1970s. For Texan trio ZZ top, Dean covered his guitars in fur: their videos, frequently filled with models, showed off the young company's guitars…

In 1986, tired of this business after just a decade, Dean Zelinsky sold his shares to Armadillo Enterprises.

After a 15-year break, Zelinsky returned to the industry as a consultant; he has since modernised his flagship model, the ML, with the new name, the Razorback, advertised as the most extreme guitar in the Dean catalogue.

Dean Razorback

Dean was inspired by Gibson to create his catalogue with the Dean V (based on the Flying V) and the Dean Z (based on the Explorer). Combining his two designs in an original and striking shape, two years later, he produced the Dean ML (as a tribute to his childhood friend Matt Lynn).

The Razorback, co-designed by Pantera guitarist Dimebag Darrell, was killed just before the Razorback was officially released in December 2004, murdered by a fan, allegedly upset by the break-up of Pantera.

A 100% heavy metal story which has no doubt contributed to the wild reputation of this guitar!

fan of Ace Frehley, the made-up guitarist of Kiss, who were his main influence. With his brother, Vinnie Paul, on the drums, he formed Pantera, a glam metal band following the heavy metal trend of the 1980s, famous for porting outfits (and haircuts) verging on the ridiculous. With the arrival of singer Phil Anselmo, the group became more aggressive and shed its trash metal image.

In 1990, their album "Cowboys from Hell" was a massive hit. But the relationship with Anselmo was deteriorating and his heroin addiction was becoming harder to manage. The band split up in 2003 after months of tension and angry exchanges between the singer and the Abbott brothers in the press. The debacle allegedly cost Dimebag Darrell his life when a deranged fan, a former marine, climbed on stage in Columbus Ohio and shot him at point-blank range along with three members of his new band Damageplan's crew.

DEFINITIVE TRACKS

| Cowboys from Hell | Pantera |
| Cemetery Gates | Pantera |

At the beginning of his glam period, **Dimebag Darrell** went by the name Diamond Darrell. His birth certificate called him Darrell Lance Abbott, and said that he was born in Arlington, Texas, on 20th August 1966. He was a great heavy metal guitarist and well known and liked for his amiable nature and rapport with fans. His father, country music singer and producer Jerry Abbott, gave him a guitar as a little boy. His first Dean was won in a talent competition organised by the manufacturer. He joined the Kiss Army as a

TRADE SECRETS

The body of the Razorback, with its pointed, spiky cutaways, is made of solid mahogany, as is the 24-fret neck, ending in a V, which was often used on Deans. The rosewood fingerboard's 12th fret was a mother-of-pearl razor blade, similar to the necklace worn by Darrell. The strident sound is achieved with two circuits: a Dimebucker (a play on words for the new humbucker made by Seymour Ducan) bridge pickup and a standard humbucker neck pickup. All the fittings are made of black anodised metal, including the double lock Floyd Rose tremolo. The guitar is available in different finishes with a range of themes including Explosion, Rebel, Camo and Cemetery Gates, a dream or a nightmare of a guitar, depending on your sensibilities!

Jackson

It all started in the early 1970s when luthier Wayne Charvel opened a little shop in Azusa, California. Charvel's Guitar Repair soon achieved a reputation for its custom guitars, but to compensate for the boss's lack of organisation, a certain Grover Jackson was hired to manage the business in exchange for a percentage of the profits.

In November 1978, Jackson offered to buy Charvel's company for $40,000. As a talented and visionary businessman, he went on to develop the brand by bringing on board the company's loyal customer, Eddie Van Halen. The long-haired hard rock guitarist had just released his band's first album on which he played a custom Charvel, the Frankenstrat.

In 1980 he had a career-changing meeting with another young heavy-metal hopeful, Randy Rhoads. Together they came up with the Randy Rhoads high-quality guitars.

Jackson was also the man to come up with the Soloist, a modernised version of the Stratocaster, with ultra powerful pickups and a 24-fret neck. Nicknamed the Superstrat, it comes in a number of ranges to suit all budgets. From the cheapest, produced in Asia, to those made individually for the brilliant, high-profile guitarists of the 1980s, including Steve Vai, Dave Mustaine (Megadeth) and Scott Ian (Anthrax). Since 2002, the Jackson/Charvel name has been taken over by Fender, who can produce as many Superstrats, inspired by its own legendary models, as it likes!

Jackson Randy Rhoads

With Randy Rhoads' asymmetric guitar, Grover launched his own Jackson brand at the turn of the 1980s. They designed the model together in just one night, with the aim of making something that wouldn't be muddled up with a Gibson Flying V. The unbalanced feel is accentuated by a longer horn pointing downwards to give it a sharp, spiky look which suited the big, saturated sound of the booming new generation of heavy metal and trash perfectly.

A great technician, Randy Rhoads revolutionised how guitars were played. Unfortunately, just as his guitar model was about to go into mass production, he died in an airplane crash when he was touring with the great Ozzy Osbourne when he was just 25 years old.

DEFINITIVE TRACKS

Crazy Train	**Ozzy Osbourne**
Mr. Crowley	**Ozzy Osbourne**

Guitar Heroes

Regarded as one of the most talented guitarists of his generation, **Randy Rhoads** started learning the guitar at his mother's music school. Some teachers refused to teach him because he was learning so fast they were worried he was becoming better than them. His first serious group was called Quiet Riot with whom he earned the title "best show in Los Angeles" and was signed to CBS. Strangely enough, the first two albums were only released in Japan in 1977 and 1978, so they're highly collectable!

The turning point of Randy Rhoads' short career came in 1979 when he was auditioned by Ozzy Osbourne. Stunned by what he heard, the former lead singer of Black Sabbath hired him on the spot. With Ozzy, Randy recorded two classic albums, "Blizzard of Oz" and "Diary of Madman". Unfortunately, it all came to an untimely end on 18th March 1982 in the middle of an American tour during a flight in a private plane that ended in a fatal crash. His brief time in the rock world turned him into a myth, highly respected by heavy metal fans. The Rhoads guitar, which he designed and created, keeps his innovative spirit alive.

© Ross Halfin-Idols/DALLE

TRADE SECRETS

The Randy Rhoads is a solid body guitar, directly inspired by the shape of Gibson's Flying V. The body is made of alder with a flame maple sound board. The screw-on 22-fret neck has a rosewood fingerboard with mother-of-pearl "shark tooth" inlays. For the big sound, Randy chose a pair of DiMarzio pickups. A "superdistortion" for the bridge and a PAF for the neck. Reissues come with a Seymour Duncan pickup.

Like most Jackson models, the tremolo is a genuine self-locking Floyd Rose. On this Rhoads, the headstock is characteristic of the brand, at a slight angle with a pointed end and the Jackson name written along the length.

Vinnie Vincent, from Kiss, was the first guitarist to play on a Rhoads, which was given to him by Jackson after Randy's premature death.

The amps

The union of the electric guitar and its amp was formalised in 1935 with the Gibson ES-150, which came with an HE-150 amp. Early amps were tube amplifiers; over 70 years later, these are still the best. A good amp amplifies the sound produced by the guitar but also colours this sound. The tubes add a warmer colour, bringing out the harmonies of the electric signal with a natural saturation, But it's expensive and fragile technology: for the general market, it was replaced by the transistor in the 1970s. Apart from rare exceptions, like Roland's 1980s Jazz Chorus, all transistor amps, usually compact and fairly effective, to a greater or less degree, reproduce the original sound created by Fender, Fender, Vox and Marshall – in other words, the grand masters when it comes to guitars.

Jimi Hendrix, 1968.

© Sie/DALLE

Fender Twin Reverb

If you're looking for power and a clear sound, this is the Holy Grail of tube amplification: the Twin Reverb. Easy to use, all you need to do is plug in a Fender guitar to get the perfect sound and a fantastic combination.

From a young age Leo Fender was obsessed with everything to do with electronics. He fiddled about with radio amps before he even started to think about guitars. Inevitably, he produced excellent tube amps for his instruments. With the Precision bass, he designed the Bassman which was specifically designed to cope with low frequencies, and it

was immediately snapped up… by guitar players! That encouraged Leo to come up with the ideal partner for his Stratocaster. He needed a clear sound that never varies, even at full power. This resulted in the Twin in 1954.

Even with all of the knobs turned right up, its 80 watts don't produce a great deal of saturation. With no fewer than 10 tubes in the amplification chain, and two speakers, this legendary piece of kit hasn't budged in all these years. The weight of the Twin Reverb hasn't changed either, at a very compact 30kg!

Vox AC30

This is the mythical amp of English rock, and produced an ample, striking sound. It is especially effective at full volume, when the shimmering tubes get the perfect level of saturation, which was made popular by The Beatles, The Kinks, The Who and the Rolling Stones, and then later by Queen, The Jam and U2.

After the Second World War, Tom Jennings produced the Univox electronic organ. In 1956, friends Dick Denney brought him a prototype for a guitar amp that they called the Vox AC15. The amp was quickly adopted for live performances by British pop bands like The Shadows. Guitarist, Hank Marvin, armed with his Stratocaster, wanted more: he urged the English company to increase his amp's power. In 1960, the extra watts that he'd so wanted were included in the Vox AC30. A touch of genius, with its 11 incandescent tubes, and the Top Boost feature added even more brilliance.

Marshall JMC800

This brilliant creation was produced by the Marshall workshops in the 1980s. Its innovative feature was a preamp (boost channel) that can be adjusted to change the level of saturation and has a separate master volume button too. For rock music, it is the ultimate tube amplifier, producing a smouldering, timeless sound.

Jim Marshall owned a shop in London where he gave drumming lessons and repaired amps. By taking them apart, he learnt how they worked and designed the legendary JTM45 in 1962, the definitive blues rock amp, which was quickly adopted by Eric Clapton to use with his Gibson Les Paul.

In 1965, The Who's guitarist, Pete Townshend, wanted a really big amp for his Gibson SG, so Jim had the idea of separating the main unit and the speakers into two to make them easier to transport. And so the Stack was born.

Roadies are still grateful to him today! The Marshall 200 watts was created at the request of Ritchie Blackmore for Deep Purple's big, hard rock sound. The icon wanted something that no Marshall amp had ever given a musician. The boss insisted that quality should be paid for, and he never deviated from that, even when it came to demands from rock legends.

One day, a cocky guy came along with his Stratocaster. He tried out all the amps in the shop, and left with four 100 watt Marshall Stacks, without asking for any discount at all. It was Jimi Hendrix.

Those who know about these things will tell you that no two amps sound the same. The quality or the level of wear of the tubes can change everything. So, just two tips: try it first…. and play it loud!

The effects pedals

Effects pedals were invented in the 1960s, initially to avoid having to adjust the settings on the amps. Before long, they made it possible to produce a wide range of sounds. These small electronic units are plugged into the guitar and the amp and are controlled by gentle pressure from the guitarist's foot on a pedal. The pedals can be plugged in separately or together: distortion, delay, chorus, flanger, wah-wah... more than enough to satisfy the most creative musicians.

Big Muff

The best known fuzz pedal was created by Electro-Harmonix in 1970. A simple square box with three control knobs for sustain, tone and volume. At the time, it was a popular effect with Pink Floyd's David Gilmour and Santana, who used it in their solos. Its creator, Mike Matthews, had designed it for his hero, Jimi Hendrix. Contrary to popular belief, the Voodoo Child never actually used the Big Muff as he died before it was released in 1971.

Seattle's grunge groups brought it back into favour in 1990; Mudhoney even paid tribute to it in their first album, "Superfuzz Bigmuff". This good old pedal, with its heavy saturation effect, was a fundamental part of the sound favoured by The White Stripes, Sonic Youth and Pantera. A customised limited edition was recently produced named after Scottish band, Mogwai, who specialise in the wall of saturated sound.

Uni-Vibe

Produced by Univox in the 1960s, this is one of Jimi Hendrix's most famous pedals. It entered the realms of rock history with *Machine Gun* and the napalm version used in *Star-Spangled Banner* as played at Woodstock: two protests against the Vietnam war. This effect, somewhere between vibrato and chorus, was actually meant to simulate the sound produced by a Leslie speaker normally used with organs. Its designer, John Mayer, who made effects pedals for Hendrix, tells the story of when Jimi talked about sounds like a painter talks about colours, to conjure up emotions. His gouache palette including Octavia, Uni-Vibe, Wah-Wah and Fuzz-Face, all plugged into his Stratocaster and his Marshall amp.

Wah-wah

The wah-wah effect started out as a mute for jazz trumpeters. Engineers tried to imitate the sound of a muted trumpet by creating the wah-wah pedal for electric guitars. The system involves a filter that changes the frequency using a pedal. Legend has it that it was Frank Zappa who introduced the wah-wah effect to Jimi Hendrix in 1967. The latter used it to great effect on *Voodoo Child (Slight Return)*.

It has been used in the psychedelic world of Eric Clapton during his Cream period, in jazz rock with Miles Davis, and in soul music with Isaac Hayes (listen to his famous *Theme from Shaft* for an example).

Vox didn't apply for a patent for its invention so many models are in circulation. The pedals by Morley and Jim Dunlop are among the more reliable.

Fuzz-Tone

It was quite by accident that a guitar was recorded with a distorted sound in 1960 with *Don't Worry about Me* by Marty Robbins, because of a fault amp. After that, The Ventures tried to reproduce the effect with the first Fuzz-Tone pedal on *2000 Pound Bee* in 1962. But the first real hit with a saturated sound came two years later with The Kinks

and *You Really Got Me*, which was achieved with a little amp whose speaker cone had been slashed by guitarist Dave Davies. Keith Richards would use a Fuzz-Tone pedal with the Stones on *(I Can't Get No) Satisfaction* in May 1965.

In the UK, stocks of these pedals sold out in a matter of months!

Tube Screamer

The very first TS 808 from Ibanez, easily recognisable from its green colour, arrived in the 1970s in the midst of the punk movement. As the name suggests, it provides a vintage sound, saturating the tubes, which was popular with slightly linear transistor amps.

Its resilient sturdiness made the Tube Screamer a standard with rockers, from the most obscure, like Gibus, to the best known veterans like Carlos Santana and the late great Stevie Ray Vaughan.

Glossary

Accessories: accessories and spare parts which are attached to the body of a guitar.

Acoustic: instrument equipped with a sound box to naturally amplify the vibration of the strings.

Alnico: an acronym referring to metal alloys made up of aluminium (Al), nickel (Ni) and Cobalt (Co).

Archtop: acoustic guitar with a rounded soundboard, similar to that of a violin.

Bending: a technique involving pulling the string to change the tone of the note being played.

Bigsby: vibrato system invented by Paul Bigsby used by a number of major guitar manufacturers

Bottleneck: cylinder, usually metal or glass, that you fit on to a finger to get a slide effect (common in blues and country music).

Bridge: part which is stuck or screwed to the body of the guitar to keep the strings in place and maintain the space between them. It helps distribute the sound waves/vibrations to the sound box.

Coil: copper coil around a magnet creating the electric circuit for a guitar pickup.

Cutaway: an indentation in the body making it easier to access the high notes at the bottom of the neck. Florentine cutaways are referred to as sharp cutaways, and Venetian cutaways as round.

Ebony: very hard, dark wood used for bridges and fingerboards.

Electric acoustic: an acoustic guitar fitted with an amplifying device.

Feedback: the Larsen effect, the sound loop between the producer of the sound (speaker) and the receiver of the sound (microphone), which is characterised by a whistling noise.

F-holes: f-shaped holes in the soundboard on either side of the bridge that open up the sound coming from the sound box.

Fingerboard: thin board of hard wood stuck to the neck. The fingerboard supports the frets.

Flat top: describes acoustic guitars that have a flat sound board.

Floating bridge: part that is not fixed but rather held in place by the pressure of the strings so it can be adjusted to change the height of the strings.

Floyd Rose: vibrato system that locks the strings and prevents the guitar from going out of tune.

Fret: bars of metal that are part of the fingerboard on the neck and mark out the semitones.

Hollow body: electric guitar with a hollow body like the Gibson ES-335 or the Gretsch 6120.

Humbucker: two-coil pickup with opposite polarity to reduce interference.

Luthier: craftsman who makes, repairs and restores string instruments.

Mahogany: a reddish wood native to the tropics, used for guitar necks and bodies.

Neck: piece of wood on which the fingerboard rests with the frets and the strings. It is extended by the head of the instrument and the mechanics that keep the strings in place.

Open tuning: this involves tuning a guitar so that if strummed the strings create a chord without pressing any of the strings.

Pickguard: a protective strip to shield the sound box of the guitar from the plectrum.

Picking: the technique of playing with your fingers, popular among country and folk guitarists.

Pickup: microphone which converts the sound vibrations into electrical signals.

Rosewood: wood originally from India or Brazil that is very dense, used to make the sound box of acoustic guitars as well as the bridge and the fingerboard.

Side: the sides of the sound box, which separate the sound board from the back of the guitar.

Solid body: an electric guitar with a solid body.

Sound board: a thin piece of wood typically with f-shaped or round sound holes, which takes the vibration of the string and amplifies it via the bridge.

Sound box: body of the acoustic guitar that receives and amplifies the vibration produced by the strings.

Sound hole: a hole, usually round and decorated, located in the middle of the sound board, which opens up the sound coming from the sound box.

Spruce: wood from temperate regions, light in colour, used for sound boards for acoustic guitars.

Sunburst: Where the colour on the body of the guitar is graded a lighter colour in the centre to a darker outer colour.

Sustain: the time during which the string vibrates. The capacity of the instrument to preserve and maintain the sound of a note without the need to replay it.

Tailpiece: separate to the bridge, it anchors the strings, generally at the bottom of the sound box.

Tremolo arm: mechanical accessory attached to the bridge and/or tailpiece with a lever to vary the tension of the strings by one or more semitone at a time. Also referred to as a vibrato unit.

Truss rod: a rod running inside along the length of the neck to adjust its flexibility and the tension of the strings.

Tune-o-matic bridge: mechanical bridge made for electric guitars invented by Gibson. It is used to adjust the height of the strings separately.

X-bracing: the strips of wood fixed in the shape of a cross under the soundboard to strengthen and distribute the vibrations. Contributes to the general sound quality of the instrument.

BIBLIOGRAPHY

Le Grand Livre de la guitare
Tony Bacon (Minerva, 2004).

The Gibson Story, Julius Bellson (1973).

Blue Book of Acoustic Guitars
S. P. Fjestad – Sixth Edition
(Blue Book Publication, Inc., 1999).

*Gibson Guitars 100 Years
of an American Icon*
Walter Carter (Gibson Guitar Corporation –
General Publishing Group, Inc., 1994).

*Gretsch – The Guitars of the
Fred Gretsch Compagny*
Jay Scott (Centerstream Publishing, 1992).

Guitares
Antoine Pascal (Amateur, 2007).

Great Guitarists
Nick Freeth and Cliff Douse
(Hors Collection, 2002).

Portrait of the Blues
Paul Trynka and Val Wilmer
(Vade Retro, 1996).

Country les incontournables
Edited by Serge Loupien
(Filipacchi, 1995).

Guitares, 160 portraits de légende
Edited by Jérome Plasseraud
(Du Layeur, 2005).

*The Beatles: 1961–1970, dix années qui
ont secoué le monde Mojo magazine*
(Tournon, 2005).

Rory Gallagher
Jean-Noël Coghe
(EPM and Castor Astral, 2000).

Dylan – Portraits et témoignages
Mojo magazine (Tournon, 2006).

© Liza Krivochieine

Any documents not credited are part of the authors collections.

Design: Ramon Cucchi

Translated from French by Anna Thompson
© Apple Press

Printed and bound in China